MINISTRY OF TRUTH

ALSO BY STEVE BENEN

*The Impostors: How Republicans Quit Governing
and Seized American Politics*

MINISTRY OF TRUTH

DEMOCRACY, REALITY, AND
THE REPUBLICANS' WAR
ON THE RECENT PAST

STEVE BENEN

MARINER BOOKS
New York   Boston

HarperCollins books may be purchased for educational, business, or sales promotional use. For information, please email the Special Markets Department at SPsales@harpercollins.com.

FIRST EDITION

Library of Congress Cataloging-in-Publication Data has been applied for.

ISBN 978-0-06-339367-7

24 25 26 27 28 LBC 5 4 3 2 1

For my friends Michael and Zoe,
who hopefully know why

The party told you to reject the evidence of your eyes and ears. It was their final, most essential command.
—George Orwell, *1984*

CONTENTS

MINISTRY OF TRUTH

"WITH TIME, PEOPLE FORGET"

The Republican Party's War on the Recent Past

People in positions of authority have tried to rewrite history to suit their purposes for as long as historical records have existed. This is especially true in authoritarian regimes, which have long seen history as a malleable propaganda tool. The pattern has become tragically familiar: dictatorial powers have used their editing pens to create myths, justify decisions, erase opponents, and even dispose of crimes.

As modern Republican politics becomes increasingly radicalized, it's not too surprising to see the party read from a similarly despotic script. Indeed, the party has invested a considerable amount of time and effort into rewriting the parts of American history that fail to suit its purposes. Textbooks and historical details have become key elements of the GOP's culture war crusade, as assorted partisans take aim at the events of decades and centuries ago as part of an unsettling and nationalistic attempt at historical revisionism.

What's less appreciated is the fact that those are not the only stories from our collective history that the party has been desperate to rewrite.

Just as important as Republicans targeting events from generations past is the GOP's war on the *recent* past, as the party wages frantic gaslighting campaigns to rewrite the stories that have unfolded over the last several years, molding the developments into unrecognizable new accounts.

With unnerving frequency, the contemporary Republican Party sees the recent past as an enemy to be overpowered, crushed, and conquered. It's an effort predicated on the assumption that our memories can be bullied into submission, forced to give way to manufactured stories the GOP prefers.

To see such authoritarian tactics in American democracy as anything less than dangerous would be a mistake. The more Republicans take aim at the public's understanding of recent events, the more dramatic the impact on everything from the public discourse to policymaking to the integrity of democracy itself.

On the surface, such mendacious campaigns have the appearance of typical, albeit brazen, dishonesty. But just below the surface, a more noxious strategy comes into focus. Leading GOP voices aren't just lying; they're also manufacturing narratives, hoping to replace accurate stories the party finds inconvenient, embarrassing, or both.

What's more, many of the routine political lies that dot our landscape are not always immediately obvious. They become evident only after the fact, by way of fact-checking analysis. The war on the recent past, however, asks people to ignore what they already saw, learned, and experienced, replacing those memories with malign myths.

The motivations behind such campaigns are hardly subtle. The more recent events can be altered to fit a political agenda, the easier it becomes to present failures as triumphs and fiction as fact. What's more, scandals and investigations can be made to disappear just as soon as a party agrees to tell its supporters that it's been exonerated—even when the opposite is true.

This campaign of rewriting recent history is built on a foundation of pernicious pillars. The first is a wholesale indifference toward reality. If a skirmish in this conflict is going to succeed, its warriors must make a deliberate choice not to care about what the public already knows to be true or what independent fact-checkers are going to say when the dust clears.

The second is the absence of shame. Campaigns to rewrite recent history fail if those doing the rewriting express a degree of embarrassment, betraying their mendacious goals. The public will pick up on sheepishness, so Republicans who intend to replace a factual series of events with fictional ones must fully commit to the new narrative, no matter how ridiculous it is.

The third is the role of allies. No one person, no matter how powerful or politically influential, can rewrite history on his or her own. The GOP's war on the recent past relies on a comprehensive approach, incorporating conservative media allies and like-minded partisans willing to echo the preferred, made-up story.

Indeed, it's this point that helps separate contemporary propaganda efforts from their predecessors: Republican officials can rely on Fox News and related outlets to help disseminate their rewritten stories—quickly and efficiently, exploiting the partisan benefits of information bubbles—in ways previous parties would've envied.

Finally, there's the importance of repetition. Recent history isn't rewritten overnight. It takes a sustained effort, reinforced over time. In his 1938 book, *Propaganda Boom*, British author A. J. Mackenzie emphasized the importance of repetition in a successful propaganda campaign, and nearly a century later that hasn't changed.

Taken together, a picture emerges of a Republican Party that's grown reliant on a brute-force rhetorical strategy, taking developments that unfolded in recent memory and replacing them with a politically advantageous alternate reality.

To be sure, Crisis Management 101 is filled with familiar lessons for parties and politicians caught up in dilemmas of varying degrees of seriousness. The rhetorical ploys are tried and true: Countless actors have done their best to put a positive spin on difficult circumstances. Others have peddled dubious denials. Some have come clean while begging the electorate for forgiveness, while others still have tried to change the subject, hoping to get away with transgressions by giving the public something else to talk about.

Contemporary Republicans have launched a war on the recent past, however, for a couple of inescapable reasons. Part of the GOP's dependence is born of uniquely indefensible circumstances: too many contemporary scandals have simply proved unspinnable. It's one thing to try to change the subject in response to a routine controversy; it's something else when a White House fails spectacularly to respond to a pandemic and more than a million Americans die from a dangerous contagion.

In such instances, the Crisis Management playbook sits on a shelf. It's not enough to simply try to negate such controversies through traditional public relations tactics; it becomes necessary to overhaul the canonical understanding of what actually transpired.

GOP voices also have grown dependent on this approach because they've found that rewriting recent history can be incredibly effective. Rank-and-file Republican voters have been conditioned to distrust independent sources of information, and with the help of allied far-right outlets, the party now believes, with good cause, that counternarratives can become the prevailing accounts—at least among those the GOP relies on for support, money, and votes.

Such tactics have become a staple of Republican politics in the era of Donald Trump—including his final full day in the Oval Office.

Presidential farewell addresses hold a special place in the American tradition. George Washington voiced fears over factionalism in 1796, for example, and those concerns remain a staple of history classes more than two centuries later. Similarly, Dwight Eisenhower's warnings of a "military-industrial complex" in 1961 quickly entered the nation's political lexicon and remain highly relevant.

To the extent that Trump's farewell address on January 19, 2021, will be remembered, it's unlikely to be held in such high regard.

As the Republican prepared to relinquish power, the outgoing president spoke under extraordinary and historically unprecedented circumstances. A week earlier, Trump had been impeached by a bipartisan majority in the U.S. House. The week before that, an insurrectionist mob attacked the U.S. Capitol at his behest, sparking conversations among his own Cabinet members about removing Trump from office by way of the Twenty-Fifth Amendment.[1]

Against this backdrop, Trump delivered a twenty-minute speech in which he described a presidency that bore little resemblance to his own. It was as if his speechwriters had prepared a farewell address for someone else entirely.

Early in his remarks, the departing president called on Americans to "rise above the partisan rancor," which seemed oddly comical given the broader context and the degree to which Trump spent his term creating a toxic political environment. But just as notably, he took the opportunity to effectively rewrite the story of his own presidency, presenting details of his supposed record that were plainly at odds with what had transpired over the previous four years.

The Republican declared with pride that he was responsible for creating "the greatest economy in the history of the world," which wasn't even close to being true.[2] He boasted that he'd signed into law "the largest package of tax cuts" in American history, which was also plainly false.[3]

In the same speech, Trump claimed credit for an ambitious health care program for veterans, which had actually been created by Barack Obama years earlier.[4]

Perhaps most important, the outgoing president assured the American public that, thanks to his leadership, "The world respects us again." In an apparent message for Joe Biden, the day before the Democrat's inauguration, Trump added, "Please don't lose that respect."

In reality, extensive public-opinion research conducted

around the globe confirmed that during Trump's presidency, respect for and confidence in the United States had collapsed to a degree unseen since the dawn of modern polling.[5]

The picture the soon-to-be-former president was eager to present as he exited the White House was an obvious and demonstrable sham. Americans were treated to a farewell address in which Trump, unable to celebrate what actually transpired during his scandal-plagued term, described accomplishments that existed only in his mind.

There was a thematic symmetry to the circumstances. On his first full day as president, Trump bragged that it did not rain at his 2017 inauguration, despite the fact that the public saw attendees in raincoats getting wet.[6] It stood to reason that on his last full day in office, he'd end his tenure with another don't-believe-your-lying-eyes pitch to the public.

Listening to the remarks was, by any fair measure, a bewildering experience. But the speech was also emblematic of the larger phenomenon plaguing contemporary Republican politics.

As 2023 neared its end, national public-opinion surveys found that a majority of Republican voters believed[7] that Trump made no effort to overturn the 2020 election; the former president did not keep classified documents at his Mar-a-Lago venue; the January 6 attack on the Capitol did not deserve to be seen as an insurrectionist riot; and the January 6 assault was not perpetrated by those intent on keeping Trump in power.

It's not an accident that such an enormous chunk of the American electorate would get each of these issues so completely wrong. To grasp why so many GOP voters have gotten reality backward, it's important to understand the strategy that left them misinformed.

The party occasionally put these narrative-reconstruction efforts to good use during the Obama era. In 2013, for example, Republicans thought they had, at long last, uncovered a legitimate scandal surrounding the Obama White House. According to the GOP's initial narrative, the Democratic administration had been caught using the Internal Revenue Service to "target" conservatives, which was characterized as an obvious and outrageous abuse of power. Among conservatives on Capitol Hill, comparisons to Richard Nixon's notorious Watergate scandal quickly became commonplace.

At least for a few days, the matter appeared rather serious, right up until the controversy evaporated. A closer review found that the tax agency scrutinized liberal, conservative, and nonideological groups with equal vigor, effectively ending the story.[8] Every relevant allegation, including conspiracy theories about White House involvement, was thoroughly discredited.

Congressional Republicans spent the ensuing two years searching for evidence of systemic wrongdoing, but to no avail. GOP lawmakers claimed to have found instances in which some conservative groups faced tougher scrutiny from some within the IRS, but despite their best efforts, Republicans found no proof to bolster their apoplexy. Similarly, the FBI launched its own probe, and federal law enforcement didn't uncover anything, either.[9] A federal prosecutor also examined the allegations and found no lines had been crossed.[10] The IRS's inspector general's office conducted its own investigation and came to a similar conclusion.[11] The "scandal," such as it was, proved to be a mirage.

So, Republicans rewrote the story.

In the revised version of what transpired, party leaders took the original details, scrapped the conclusion, wrote a new final chapter, and hoped the political world wouldn't notice the difference. In the rewritten story, the original controversy remained entirely intact, and the results of the thorough investigations were simply ignored.

In 2016, for example, Representative Ron DeSantis— before he ran for Senate, governor, and later, president— launched an impeachment push targeting IRS commissioner John Koskinen, accusing him of a variety of imagined misdeeds related to the discredited scandal. The Florida Republican, not coincidentally, also used the crusade as part of a lucrative fundraising effort,[12] helping DeSantis fill his campaign coffers ahead of his bids for higher office.

In the years that followed, the GOP did its best to keep the myth alive, putting its revised version of the controversy to use in 2021, as the Biden White House and Republican leaders engaged in difficult discussions over a proposed infrastructure package. Republican officials insisted that they'd oppose any compromise that asked anyone to pay more in taxes, and the Democratic president grudgingly accepted the fact that GOP lawmakers would not budge on this point. But in the interest of keeping the process moving forward, Biden instead offered an alternative: the IRS could simply better enforce the tax laws already on the books, collecting new revenues that could go toward the nation's infrastructure needs, without raising anyone's taxes at all.

Republicans balked at this, too. Senator John Cornyn of Texas, for example, said the party couldn't accept such an approach because the IRS "has a reputation problem because of weaponization." He specifically pointed to the faux scandal from 2013.[13]

The senator had plenty of company. When far-right groups started lobbying Congress[14] against the IRS provision in the infrastructure deal, they sent a letter to senators that read in part, "No additional funding for the Internal Revenue Service, especially given its multiple scandals over the past decade." The letter specifically claimed that the agency had "harassed conservative groups and donors," despite reality.

A member of the editorial board of the *Wall Street Journal*, a reliable GOP ally, pushed the same line,[15] insisting that the IRS had "unfairly singled out conservative non-profits for special scrutiny and harassment." The opinion piece, unconcerned by the evidence, added, "It was a sobering lesson in how one of Washington's most powerful agencies can be weaponized against political opponents."

The claims weren't true—effectively every aspect of the controversy had been disproven—but they had the intended effect, and improved enforcement of federal tax laws was not included in the final bipartisan infrastructure deal.

It captured one of the central problems with the GOP's misinformation strategy: the effects aren't philosophical, they're practical. Republicans rewrote the essential details of an important story; the twisted version of reality took root; and it was still hindering the government's core functions long after the truth faded from the front pages.

A year later, in the wake of the 2022 midterm elections,

House GOP leader Kevin McCarthy struggled to an excruciating degree to secure the votes he needed from his own party to become House speaker. Hoping to impress the Republican conference, McCarthy unveiled a blueprint highlighting the kind of investigations he'd help launch in the next Congress if he were put in charge of the chamber.[16]

Halfway through the list was a predictable reference to the Internal Revenue Service. "The Democrats have politicized the IRS at every turn," the future House speaker wrote, pointing to developments that never actually occurred. McCarthy added, as if on cue, that Obama administration officials, nearly a full decade earlier, "intentionally targeted conservative leaning non-profit organizations in an attempt to silence political speech they disagreed with."

The fact that this hadn't happened was beside the point, since the myth had become a touchstone on the political right. The GOP leader was eager to find common cause with his party's far-right members, while demonstrating a commitment to their favorite legends. Naturally, McCarthy turned to one of the stories Republicans had worked so hard to rewrite.

There was no great mystery as to why this was such a priority for the party and its allies: The GOP is an avowed antitax party that sees political utility in demonizing the government agency responsible for collecting tax revenue. Any myth villainizing the IRS remained potent, so its leaders put it to use.

At that point, the established pattern kicked in. Republicans took an existing story—at least initially, there were some legitimate questions about how the IRS treated groups seeking tax-exempt status—and decided to brush aside the inconvenient factual details or the results of multiple investigations. The party proceeded to shamelessly pretend that its version of the scandal was real, relied on like-minded allies to help undermine the facts that the public might remember, and repeated the revised story ad nauseam.

Years later, it's become an article of faith in GOP circles that the IRS was caught red-handed discriminating against mistreated conservative victims, reality be damned.

But while Americans saw battles like these in the war on the recent past during Obama's presidency, it was Trump who took the conflict to unsettling depths, leaning on the ploy throughout his term in the hopes that rewriting stories would help get him out of assorted messes he'd created for himself.

In the wake of his election victory in 2016, for example, Trump was annoyed by the results of the popular vote, which he handily lost. The electoral college results dictated the outcome, but the fact remained that when American voters were given a choice between him and Hillary Clinton, the former Democratic secretary of state finished with nearly 3 million more votes than her GOP rival.

Uncomfortable with such details, Trump rewrote the story. Despite the unambiguous results that the public was well aware of, just weeks after Election Day, the president-elect used social media to deride what he characterized as the "so-called popular vote,"[17] which Trump said he secretly won by way of evidence he could never produce.

It was deeply strange for a winning candidate to publicly question the reliability of an election that he'd won, but Trump kept adding delusional chapters to his revised story, indifferent to the fact that the vast majority of observers already knew the truth. On his fourth day in office, the Republican hosted a White House event with congressional leaders from both parties and both chambers, at which point he needlessly relitigated the race he'd won a few months earlier, insisting that "illegals"—a slur used by the right to refer to undocumented immigrants—deprived him of a victory in the popular vote by casting several million improper ballots.[18]

The claim was preposterous, as the president's own lawyers conceded in a court filing during the postelection transition period.[19] But the true story—Clinton won the popular vote by a comfortable margin—embarrassed Trump, so he kept facts that were plainly true at arm's length while simultaneously making up new ones.

In fact, when Democratic leaders at the White House meeting gently reminded the president of what had actually happened, Trump presented lawmakers with what he characterized as credible evidence:[20] A professional golfer named Bernhard Langer, according to the president, told him that he was in line to vote at a polling place in Florida but was denied a ballot. According to the same strange story, Langer added that he saw others he suspected were noncitizens who were permitted to cast provisional ballots.

According to a *New York Times* report, the anecdote was "greeted with silence, and Mr. Trump was prodded to change the subject by Reince Priebus, the White House chief of staff." (The golfer is a German citizen who can't vote in the United States. Langer's daughter denied that her father and the Republican were friends.[21])

The gathering came just two days after Trump—not quite twenty-four hours into his presidency—personally called the head of the National Park Service and directed him to produce flattering evidence regarding the size of the crowd at his inauguration.[22] The Republican, mortified by the paltry turnout for his swearing-in ceremony, saw the story of his audience as another tale in need of a tweak.

After Park Service officials sent additional photographs that confirmed reality and challenged the president's assumptions, Trump deployed the White House press secretary, Sean Spicer, to the briefing room to tell reporters, "This was the largest audience to ever witness an inauguration—period."[23]

The rhetoric was as ludicrous as it was unnecessary.[24] While some of the Republican's whoppers required some research and analysis before being exposed as lies, this was an instance in which cameras, just two days earlier, captured the modest crowds and empty bleachers along the Pennsylvania Avenue parade route. There was no point in telling Americans they didn't see what they thought they saw.

In the war on the recent past, Spicer proved to be a discomfited field general: after leaving his White House post, the former presidential spokesperson told NPR that he wished he could get "a do-over" on the comments.[25]

While Spicer's rhetoric became the stuff of late-night punch lines, far less amusing was Trump's willingness to try to rewrite the events in Charlottesville, Virginia, in 2017. After a white nationalist event turned deadly—a self-proclaimed neo-Nazi used his car to murder thirty-two-year-old Heather Heyer and injure dozens of other counterprotesters—the Republican president condemned[26] the "egregious display of hatred, bigotry, and violence—on many sides, on many sides."

The rhetoric suggested that Trump was not only eager to avoid criticizing racists directly, he also saw a moral equivalence between white supremacists and their opponents, as if both were equally culpable for what transpired. Facing an avalanche of angry responses, the president managed to dig deeper a couple of days later, responding to the pushback by defending some of the racist activists, telling reporters, "Not all of those people were neo-Nazis, believe me. Not all of those people were white supremacists by any stretch."

Trump concluded that there were "very fine people on both sides."[27]

As the Republican's rhetoric became notorious, the president again took aim at the events in the hopes of relitigating his own scandalous comments. "If you look at what I said, you will see that that question was answered perfectly," he told reporters.[28] "I was talking about people that went [to Charlottesville] because they felt very strongly about the monument to Robert E. Lee, a great general. Whether you like it or not, he was one of the great generals. I have spoken to many generals here, right at the White House, and many people thought—of the generals, they think that he was maybe their favorite general."

Trump concluded, "People were there protesting the taking down of the monument of Robert E. Lee. Everybody knows that."

What "everybody" actually knew was something altogether different. The Republican wasn't simply defending fans of a Robert E. Lee statue: the "very fine people" whom Trump was eager to support were the same people chanting, among other things, "Jews will not replace us" and "Blood and soil."[29]

Trump's motivation for trying to amend his own record was entirely straightforward: his rhetoric about events in Charlottesville proved to be one of the bigger fiascos of his first year in office. Former allies abandoned the Republican in the aftermath of the controversy—there was an exodus of private-sector leaders who resigned from White House boards,[30] no longer wanting to be associated with Trump—and the scandal even affected his private-sector enterprise, as the president's glorified country club at Mar-a-Lago faced cancellations[31] fueled by his "very fine people" rhetoric.

But the reasoning behind the rewrite didn't make the public relations effort any less offensive. The gut-wrenching violence in Charlottesville jolted the nation, and Heyer's death was a tragedy felt far and wide. It was a moment that called for an empathic leader to step up, prioritize national unity and respect for diversity, and at least try to advance the cause of healing. Trump did the opposite, not only by rewriting the story of his role, but also by doing so in a way that enflamed the situation and lent tacit support to extremists.

The GOP's focus on the events of generations past has become a staple of contemporary Republican politics. Literally the day before Election Day 2020, for example, Trump signed an executive order establishing what the White House described as the "1776 Commission."[32] Explaining its value, the president said the initiative would help "clear away the twisted web of lies in our schools and classrooms," adding that versions of history at odds with conservatives' values constituted "a form of child abuse."[33]

His executive order added, "Despite the virtues and accomplishments of this Nation, many students are now taught in school to hate their own country, and to believe that the men and women who built it were not heroes, but rather villains."

The commission featured no professional historians, and it showed. On Trump's last full day as president, the White House panel released an inconsequential forty-five-page report—the document, among other things, endorsed a far-right vision that blamed historical ills on the left, while warning the public about the perils of a so-called administrative state[34]—that was widely panned by qualified scholars.

James Grossman, the executive director of the American Historical Association, described the commission's findings as a work of "cynical politics," adding, "This report skillfully weaves together myths, distortions, deliberate silences, and both blatant and subtle misreading of evidence to create a narrative and an argument that few respectable professional historians, even across a wide interpretive spectrum, would consider plausible, never mind convincing."[35]

Grossman went on to say, in reference to the Republican endeavor, "They're using something they call history to stoke culture wars."

It was hardly an isolated incident. Two years later, Florida's state Board of Education approved new African American history standards that said students should learn that slaves in the United States "developed skills which, in some instances, could be applied for their personal benefit."[36]

The suggestion that some Black people benefited from slavery—as if there are upsides to crimes against humanity—sparked an immediate and unavoidable outcry, though it wasn't the only odious element in the standards. Kevin Kruse, a history professor at Princeton University, wrote a related analysis,[37] highlighting several elements of the standards that reflected "the clumsy influence of partisan politics."

Kruse found that members of the state Board of Education—handpicked by Ron DeSantis, whose GOP presidential campaign struggled to address the debacle—approved history standards that needlessly elevated conservative and Republican figures while simultaneously referencing a civil rights law that doesn't exist.

Board members defended the standards by pointing to sixteen individuals who, they claimed, developed valuable skills while enslaved. The *New York Times'* Jamelle Bouie explained soon after that the rejoinder was roughly as flawed as the standards themselves: "Several of the people cited weren't ever enslaved, and there's little evidence that those who were learned any relevant skills for their 'personal benefit' in slavery."[38]

The uproar coincided with revelations that DeSantis's administration also approved materials created by an outfit called PragerU, a nonprofit organization cofounded by a conservative radio host. A *Tampa Bay Times* investigation concluded, "The content—some of which is narrated by conservative personalities such as Candace Owens and Tucker Carlson—features cartoons, five-minute video history lessons and story-time shows for young children and is part of a brand called PragerU Kids. And the lessons share a common message: Being pro-American means aligning oneself to mainstream conservative talking points."[39]

The uncomfortable fact remains, however, that while

rewriting the history of generations past is menacing, Republicans and their allies have also found it relatively easy. Most people are not scholars. They do not have history degrees. Their understanding of people and events that predate their lifetimes is susceptible to manipulation.

One of the PragerU videos, for example, featured an animated Booker T. Washington distorting the history of the Civil War, including a voice actor saying things the iconic educator never said and endorsing ideas belied by Washington's genuine vision.[40] A typical person might not immediately recognize the flaws in the content, and many students being presented the information in a school setting would likely believe it.

Rewriting events from the recent past, however, requires a different kind of audacity and ambition. At issue are events most Americans saw and remember. These aren't subjects of debate for historical symposiums, or obscure developments that an average person might have a superficial understanding of. Rather, at issue are events from the last few years that people lived through and experienced firsthand.

Republicans have nevertheless taken on the bold challenge of convincing people that their eyes have deceived them; their memories are wrong; independent sources of information are not to be trusted; and partisan changes to the recent past deserve to be embraced without question.

It reflects a radical vision that Trump and his allies have imposed on Republican politics. This is, after all, the party of "alternative facts."[41] And "polls are fake, just like everything else."[42] "Truth isn't truth."[43] "Over time, facts develop"[44] and its rhetorical cousin, facts "are in the eye of the beholder."[45]

The point is not that the Democratic Party is filled exclusively with angels who would never dare to consider putting a misleading spin on mortifying missteps. Most fair-minded observers know better. But the qualitative difference between the parties is unavoidable. It didn't occur to Obama and his White House team to tell the public that the Affordable Care Act's website worked flawlessly from the start, and anyone who says otherwise is promoting a lie. It also didn't occur to Hillary Clinton to launch a mind-numbing crusade based on the idea that she'd secretly won the electoral college vote in 2016, pointing to evidence of systemic fraud that existed only in her mind.

Such mendacity would've immediately been recognized as outlandish, which was why the party and its leaders saw no value in even trying to peddle such absurdities. In GOP politics, however, there are no comparable reservations.

As Trump's first year in the White House neared an end, Billy Bush, to whom the Republican bragged about assaulting women during the infamous *Access Hollywood* recording,[46] wrote an opinion piece for the *New York Times* explaining what he'd learned about the president.

After noting that he'd confronted Trump about inflating the ratings of his reality-television program, *The Apprentice*, Bush wrote that Trump had told him privately, "People will just believe you. You just tell them, and they believe you."[47]

Years later, the Republican and his party adopted an eerily similar approach to describing the details of key events from our collective recent history, based in part on the expectation that Americans "will just believe" them.

It's a vision that has come to define the former president's approach to communicating with the public. In the summer of 2023, Trump used his social media platform to declare with enthusiasm, "With time, people forget!"[48] What might have seemed like a complaint was better seen as a problem that Trump and his party have been eager to exploit in dangerous ways.

When George Orwell wrote *1984* in the aftermath of World War II, the hero of his novel, Winston Smith, works for the ruling party's propaganda arm. It was called the Ministry of Truth, and it was responsible for, among other things, rewriting history. Among the lessons Smith was told to embrace was the notion that "the past was alterable."

It's a principle the former president and his party have embraced with unnerving enthusiasm.

This book is not intended as a comprehensive review of American politics from the last several years. What's more, many of the underlying events are themselves familiar—the January 6 attack, the federal response to the Covid pandemic, Trump's impeachments, et al.—and those stories won't be retold in granular detail here.

Rather, the book is intended as a lens through which to see GOP misinformation campaigns, contextualizing partisan efforts that were, and are, intended to convince people they do not remember the events Republicans would prefer they forget.

The point is to shine a spotlight on how the Republican Party has tried to rewrite our recent history, why the GOP has grown so dependent on the tactic, the degree to which the partisan campaigns have succeeded, and the consequences of the party's alternative narratives challenging reality.

"All authoritarian movements know the power of historical myths," the *Washington Post*'s Max Boot wrote in early 2021.[49] "That's why they go to such great lengths to rewrite the past to justify their rule. . . . The Republican Party, as it becomes increasingly anti-democratic, is no different. It is busy reshaping both the distant past and the more recent past to its liking."

The stakes couldn't be much higher: The foundation of democracy rests in large part on a shared understanding of current events. When that understanding is deliberately corrupted by brazen partisans, the consequences can be dire.

The more Republicans attack the recent past, the more a larger political crime comes into view: the party increasingly sees the tools that the electorate relies on to make sound decisions—facts, memories, records, an ability to apply lessons learned—as little more than annoyances to be discarded. To allow the GOP to succeed is to tolerate an offensive that's pushing our political system to the breaking point.

CHAPTER 1

"RUSSIA, RUSSIA, RUSSIA"

Rewriting the Story of the Trump/Russia Scandal

In August 2022, Donald Trump's legal difficulties reached a new and startling level. FBI officials executed a court-approved search warrant at Mar-a-Lago, in the hopes of retrieving classified materials the Republican took from the White House after his election defeat, and in the process, the public came to realize that he'd likely soon become the first former American president to be indicted on felony charges.

House Republican Conference chair Elise Stefanik was among the many GOP voices who scrambled to defend Trump, despite the extensive evidence pointing to his apparent guilt, and she settled on a specific line of argument designed to appeal to her fellow partisans.

"This is Russia hoax 2.0," the New York congresswoman said.[1]

Several months later, after Trump was indicted in Manhattan as part of his hush-money-to-a-porn-star scandal,

Stefanik again returned to her go-to talking point. The charges, she wrote via social media, were part of an "unconstitutional pattern going back to the illegal Russian collusion hoax."[2]

Former vice president Mike Pence thought along the same lines, arguing that the investigation in New York "reeks of the kind of political prosecution that we endured back in the days of the Russia hoax."[3]

Pence and Stefanik didn't elaborate. For Republicans, they didn't have to. A shorthand of sorts had already become ubiquitous in GOP circles: Trump had faced allegations of "collusion" with Russia, but the scandal was thoroughly discredited; the former president was completely exonerated; and the underlying controversy was exposed as a "hoax."

With these assumptions having been widely embraced by partisans, it wasn't long before Trump and his allies started applying their supposition to the Republican's other unrelated problems. In December 2022, for example, the former president used his social media platform to make the case that his fictional claims about systemic voter fraud in the 2020 race were not only true, they were so significant that they "allow for the termination of all rules, regulations, and articles, even those found in the Constitution."[4]

When the missive sparked a controversy, Trump wrote another message saying the pushback was "simply more DISINFORMATION & LIES, just like RUSSIA, RUSSIA, RUSSIA."[5] Similarly, when the New York attorney general's office accused the Trump Organization of fraudulent business practices on a systemic scale, the former president declared, "This is like Russia, Russia, Russia, which turned out to be a hoax."[6] When a bipartisan congressional committee unveiled its findings on an investigation into the January 6 attack, he added that the panel's members were not to be trusted— because they believed "the RUSSIA, RUSSIA, RUSSIA HOAX."[7]

For Trump and his cohorts, the line was effectively a get-out-of-trouble-free card, to be played ad nauseam: if the Russia scandal wasn't real, then voters should necessarily discount every other controversy related to the former president, whether that made sense or not.

"Every time you see these Radical Lunatics and their partners in the Fake News Media talking about the 'Trials and Tribulations' of President Donald Trump, please remember that it is all a coordinated HOAX, just like Russia, Russia, Russia," Trump wrote in July 2023.[8]

Part of the problem with this line of argument is the inherent logical fallacy: if people are falsely accused of wrongdoing, it doesn't mean they're innocent against all other accusations. But in this specific instance, there was a far more important problem: the GOP rhetoric was predicated on the idea that Trump's Russia scandal was proven baseless.

Reality told a very different story, despite Republican efforts to rewrite it.

There were signs of potential trouble long before Trump went anywhere near the West Wing. In December 2015, the future president was asked about Russia's Vladimir Putin and his habit of invading countries and killing critics. "He's running his country, and at least he's a leader," Trump replied. Reminded that the foreign autocrat had been credibly accused of ordering the murder of critics and journalists, the Republican tried to excuse Putin's tactics by adding, "Well, I think our country does plenty of killing also."[9]

Around the same time, the then candidate signed a letter of intent to move forward with negotiations to build a Trump Tower in Russia,[10] just hours before he participated in a presidential primary debate.[11] The Republican nevertheless repeatedly told the public that he had no business dealings whatsoever in Russia.[12]

Five months later, after winning a series of GOP primaries and positioning himself as his party's likely presidential nominee, Trump delivered remarks outlining his foreign policy vision, vowing to ease "tensions" between Russia and the United States, and end "this horrible cycle of hostility."[13] The messaging did not go unnoticed. Propaganda outlets in Moscow went to unsubtle lengths to lionize the Republicans' 2016 front-runner, and *Politico* published a report in the early summer pointing to the likely GOP nominee as "the Kremlin's candidate."[14]

But a bombshell revelation in June 2016 took the controversy to a new level: Russian operatives hacked the Democratic National Committee's computer network,[15] stole materials, and then weaponized their plunder, releasing information at key intervals in the hopes of undermining Hillary Clinton's candidacy and boosting the GOP ticket.

The espionage was itself an extraordinary development. The fact that an adversary launched such an attack and targeted an American presidential election with an intelligence operation was so unprecedented that some U.S. officials treated the intrusion as the most serious domestic security breach since the terrorist attacks of September 11, 2001.[16]

The beneficiary of the Russian offensive did his best to deflect on behalf of his foreign allies. "I don't think anybody knows it was Russia that broke into the DNC," Trump said during the first of the three 2016 presidential debates.[17] Pointing to Hillary Clinton, the Republican added, "She's saying Russia, Russia, Russia, but I don't—maybe it was. I mean, it could be Russia, but it could also be China. It could also be lots of other people. It also could be somebody sitting on their bed that weighs 400 pounds, OK?"

U.S. intelligence agencies had already briefed Trump, making clear to the Republican nominee that Russia was responsible. He ignored the officials from his own country and instead embraced the Kremlin's denials. "To profess not to know at this point is willful misrepresentation," a frustrated senior U.S. intelligence official said.[18]

A month after the public learned of the Russian intelligence operation, Trump added fuel to the fire, holding a press conference in which he publicly urged the Kremlin's espionage services to further help undermine the Clinton campaign. "Russia, if you're listening, I hope you're able to find the 30,000 emails that are missing," the Republican said,[19] referencing the former secretary of state's private email server. (According to federal prosecutors, within hours of Trump's comments, the Main Intelligence Directorate in Moscow targeted Clinton's personal office.[20])

"There is simply no precedent for this: A presidential candidate publicly appealing to a foreign adversary to intervene in the election on his behalf," a New York Times analysis added soon after.[21]

William Inboden, who served on George W. Bush's National Security Council, described the comments as "an assault on the Constitution."[22] Michael Hayden, the former head of the National Security Agency and Central Intelligence Agency in the Bush-Cheney administration, added that Trump's rhetoric was "incredibly stunning" and "very dangerous."[23]

At this point, political observers in the United States thought they were dealing with a controversy in which Putin and his government were the principal villain for obvious reasons: it was Kremlin-backed operatives who targeted the elections with the intention of helping dictate the outcome. Though the allegations would soon be overshadowed, this initial story was seen as one of the most important campaign stories in American history.

A month after Election Day 2016, seventeen U.S. intelligence agencies released an unclassified summary of their consensus conclusions, and officials were categorical: Russia launched the operation; officials working at Putin's behest deliberately sought to subvert our democracy; and Russia was motivated in part by a desire to help put Trump in the White House.[24]

The allegations captured an almost unimaginable crime: a foreign adversary provided clandestine assistance to a man who aspired to be the leader of the free world, creating a dynamic in which the winner reached the Oval Office thanks at least in part to foreign espionage.

Josh Marshall, the editor of Talking Points Memo, summarized the landscape this way: "Just two weeks before a new president is sworn into office, the country's intelligence agencies are publicly releasing a report claiming that the United States' great 20th century rival, Russia, conspired to assist in that new president's election. Step back and just absorb that. That is simply mind-boggling."[25]

At the time, there were few reasons to believe the GOP nominee and his political operation were directly involved in the scandal, aside from Trump praising and appealing to his benefactors in Moscow. But the story soon evolved into something far more pernicious: a scandal in which the Republican and his team not only benefited from Russian assistance, but also allegedly cooperated with the foreign foe's scheme.

It was on Inauguration Day 2016, literally just hours before Trump would take the oath of office, when the public learned that American law enforcement and intelligence agencies had initiated a counterintelligence investigation into suspected links between Russian officials and the incoming president's political operation.[26]

This wasn't a probe examining whether the Kremlin had targeted the elections—U.S. officials had already confirmed that it had. It was instead an investigation into whether members of Team Trump were Russia's confederates. Former FBI director Robert Mueller, a lifelong Republican, was eventually tapped to oversee the inquiry and serve as special counsel.

Soon after, the Senate Select Committee on Intelligence, led by a Republican majority, launched a separate but parallel examination of Moscow's 2016 efforts.

As the investigations unfolded, the president showed little interest in trying to shake his reputation as a leader who was a little too eager to curry favor with Moscow. In fact, retired Republican senator Dan Coats, who served for more than two years as Trump's director of national intelligence, would later concede that he believed Putin's government "had something" on Trump,[27] which left him compromised.

He wasn't the only one with such concerns. The president was so acquiescent toward Russia that former CIA director John Brennan also suggested that the Kremlin "may have something on" Trump personally.[28] Brennan added, "The Russians, I think, have had long experience with Mr. Trump, and may have things that they could expose."

Those questions grew louder in July 2018 when the Republican held a summit with Putin in Helsinki in July 2018, culminating in a disastrous press conference in which Trump sided with the Russian leader over the judgment of American intelligence professionals.[29]

Soon after, the *New York Times* reported that U.S. intelligence officials "were unanimous in saying that they and their colleagues were aghast at how Mr. Trump had handled himself with Mr. Putin."[30] One official summarized a consensus view, concluding that it was clear whose side Trump was on, and "it isn't ours."

In the aftermath of the event, Senator John McCain called Trump's appearance in Helsinki "one of the most disgraceful performances by an American president in memory."[31] The Arizona Republican, the month before his passing, went on to say, "No prior president has ever abased himself more abjectly before a tyrant."

One of Trump's former National Security Council officials was thinking along the same lines, describing the developments as "a total [effing] disgrace."[32] The same official concluded, "The president has lost his mind."

He was, however, just getting started. Trump didn't truly "lose his mind" until the investigations into his Russia scandal concluded, resulting in shocking findings that necessitated aggressive—and at times, hysterical—misinformation campaigns.

In March 2019, Mueller and his team submitted their findings to Attorney General William Barr, putting the leader of the U.S. Department of Justice in a uniquely influential position. While the party had routinely waged war against the recent past, rewriting narratives in defiance of what the public had already seen, Barr was positioned to rewrite a narrative Americans couldn't see for themselves: he had the Mueller report, and, at least initially, they didn't.

It was a dynamic the attorney general eagerly exploited. In fact, Barr initially released his own four-page summary of the special counsel's conclusions[33] rather than share the full Mueller report with the public directly. The nation's chief law enforcement official also held a press conference, putting a political spin on the special counsel's conclusions before anyone could verify whether he was telling the truth or not.

It later became clear that Barr was engaged in a partisan propaganda effort of sorts, downplaying the seriousness of Mueller's findings, and cherry-picking elements intended to help the president who'd appointed him. U.S. District Court judge Reggie Walton—a jurist chosen for the bench by George W. Bush—later slammed the attorney general for his "lack of candor" on the matter, while also calling out Barr's "distorted" and "misleading" account of Mueller's findings.[34]

Trump and his allies nevertheless seized on Barr's interpretation of Mueller's work, telling the public that the president had been fully exonerated by the special counsel's investigation. On social media, Trump published missives with the phrase "no collusion" with such frequency that he appeared to have a nervous tic.[35] A counternarrative was in place, and the party seized on it as if it had merit.

Once Mueller's report reached the public, it quickly became clear just how brazenly dishonest the White House and its allies had been about the investigation's conclusions. The special counsel's 448-page document painted a devastating picture of a president who lied and encouraged others to lie, whose political operation had "numerous links" with the Russian operatives who tried to put Trump in power, and who personally and repeatedly took a series of steps to undermine the federal criminal investigation in which he was a subject.[36]

The president, confident in his unrivaled ability to replace fact with fiction, pretended the findings were great news.

In the days and weeks after the Mueller report's release, Trump insisted that Mueller found no evidence of collusion, which was an inherently dubious claim.[37] The Republican said the investigation turned up no evidence of obstruction, which was the opposite of the truth.[38] He said the special counsel had "totally exonerated" him, which was demonstrably ridiculous.[39]

In time, Trump concocted amazing new details, including the idea that while Russians tried to "gain access" to his 2016 campaign, the Mueller report found that these foreign operatives "were rebuffed at every turn."[40] A *Washington Post* analysis described the presidential claim as "immediately, obviously and somewhat amusingly untrue,"[41] and pointed to an email Donald Trump Jr. received about the Kremlin wanting to assist his father's candidacy.

Trump Jr. replied, "If it's what you say, I love it," and a meeting at Trump Tower soon followed. No one in attendance was "rebuffed." Indeed, the *Post*'s analysis included a lengthy list of related instances in which people in the future president's orbit "rebuffed" Russians in 2016 by meeting and exploring opportunities with them.

The Senate Intelligence Committee's findings similarly did Trump and his party no favors. In fact, by some measures, it was arguably worse for Republicans than Mueller's probe.

Not only did the GOP-led committee confirm the intelligence community's assessment of Russia's attack against the U.S. political system in 2016, in a 996-page report, Senate investigators also concluded that the Trump campaign was eager to accept the assistance of a foreign adversary in the hopes of winning the White House.[42]

Perhaps most important of all, the Senate Intelligence Committee documented the extent to which Trump's campaign chairman, Paul Manafort, was in direct, frequent, and secret communication with a Russian intelligence officer throughout his tenure helming the future president's political team. The report at one point literally described a "direct tie between senior Trump Campaign officials and the Russian intelligence services."

As part of that connection, according to Senate investigators' findings, Trump's operation shared internal information with a Russian intelligence officer,[43] while amplifying the leaks of Democratic materials stolen by Kremlin-linked operatives.

The idea that the Russia scandal was a "hoax" was already impossible to take seriously, but the Intelligence Committee's findings appeared to lay waste to the talking point once and for all. Republicans couldn't even dismiss the panel's report as politically motivated because the committee was led at the time by a GOP majority.

Between the multiple investigations and reports, a handful of core truths had come into sharp relief:

1. **Russia attacked the American elections in 2016:** Every U.S. intelligence agency and the Senate Intelligence Committee agreed that the Kremlin launched an expansive and expensive covert military intelligence operation that targeted the U.S. political system in 2016.[44]

2. **Russia's goal was to put Trump in power:** The Kremlin's operation was not politically neutral; Moscow attacked our elections in the hopes of helping dictate the outcome. According to the findings of U.S. intelligence agencies, the Mueller investigation, and Senate investigators, Russia saw Trump as a prospective ally and believed it would be in its interests if the Republican were in the White House.[45]

3. **Russia and Team Trump were political allies:** While the precise meaning of the word "collusion" has long been slippery[46]—there is no legal definition, and competing players, parties, and media organizations have applied competing meanings to the term—investigators documented high-level connections between Trump's political operation and those responsible for the attack on the U.S. elections.

4. **Trump was credibly accused of obstructing the federal criminal investigation into the scandal:** While the former president spent years claiming that Mueller found "no obstruction," the special counsel documented at least ten instances in which Trump took steps to interfere with the probe.[47] When the special counsel testified on Capitol Hill in July 2019, he was explicit in telling House lawmakers that he had not cleared Trump of obstruction charges.[48]

5. **Team Trump lied about its interactions with Russia during the 2016 campaign:** Trump and members of his inner circle were categorical in their denials, insisting that no one from the team was in contact with Russians before the Republican took office in January 2017. Asked if anyone with Trump's political operation had any such contacts, Vice President Mike Pence, for example, said, "Of course not."[49] Kellyanne Conway, who served as a White House adviser to Trump, was similarly asked about the possibility of communications. She said, "Absolutely not," adding that the conversations "never happened" and any suggestions to the contrary "undermine our democracy."[50] White House Chief of Staff Reince Priebus similarly said, "Of course, we didn't interface with the Russians."[51]

Investigators ultimately pointed to Russians interacting with at least fourteen Trump associates during the campaign and presidential transition period.[52] The total number of communications totaled

more than one hundred.[53] Among them was retired
general Michael Flynn, who briefly served as Trump's
White House national security advisor before he was
fired for having lied to the FBI about his conversations with Russian officials.[54]

6. **The Russia scandal led to a series of felony convictions and prison sentences:** For an alleged "hoax,"
   the Russia scandal led to an amazing number of federal prosecutions. In fact, the investigation led to the
   convictions of, among others, Trump's White House
   national security advisor, campaign chairman, dep-
   uty campaign chairman, foreign policy advisor, and
   personal attorney,[55] and to the indictment of thir-
   teen Russian nationals who interfered in our elections as part of the larger plot.[56]

To be sure, there were elements of the scandal that remain opaque. For example, Christopher Steele, a former
British intelligence officer, was hired to prepare a dossier on
Trump's connections to Moscow, and some of his findings remain unverified. (Though Steele's core warning that Putin's
Russia was engaged in a state-sponsored influence campaign
to favor candidate Trump was borne out.)

But these six points went largely uncontested. Trump
and his team welcomed, received, benefited from, and lied
about Russian campaign assistance. Many key players from
Trump's inner circle were charged, prosecuted, and convicted. These conclusions were bolstered by multiple, bipartisan investigations, conducted across several years.

How much of this story did Republicans decide to rewrite? All of it.

There was no great mystery as to what motivated the GOP to reject the core elements of the Russia scandal. Indeed, the relevant details were brutal and impossible to spin. Team Trump cooperated with a foreign adversary while it intervened in a presidential election, then lied about it, and then obstructed an investigation. The more Americans understood what actually transpired, the more dramatic the political consequences would likely be for Trump and his party.

And so, left with limited choices, Republicans decided that reality would have to be replaced. In the new story, Team Trump had nothing to do with its Russian benefactors, and the real scandal was a group of out-of-control investigators who manufactured a "hoax" out of thin air.

In fact, in the aftermath of the investigations, Trump and his allies took aim at even the most basic details. During his 2020 reelection campaign, for example, the incumbent president told Fox Business that he'd heard that Russian operatives targeted the 2016 election because "they wanted Hillary Clinton to win."[57]

After his defeat, Trump used his newfound free time to complain about the *New York Times* and the *Washington Post* having received Pulitzer Prizes for their 2018 coverage of the Russia scandal.[58] The former president apparently thought it'd be a good idea to appeal to the Pulitzer Prize board, asking its members to reverse course and strip the newspapers of the honor because, according to the story the Republican wanted people to believe, the awards were in recognition of reporting on a scandal that had been discredited.

In an exceedingly generous move, the Pulitzer board took Trump's appeals seriously, indulged his fantasy, and launched independent reviews of the newspapers' reporting. Predictably, they found that the *Times* and the *Post* were right,[59] and none of the reporting had been debunked.

Around the same time, the former president inexplicably thought it'd be wise to sue Hillary Clinton and several other prominent Democrats, claiming that they tried to rig the 2016 presidential election by bringing attention to his Russia scandal.[60] The case alleged "racketeering" and a "conspiracy to commit injurious falsehood," and it presented "a veritable smorgasbord of debunked and conspiratorial assertions" as evidence.[61]

When the case reached U.S. District Court Judge Donald Middlebrooks, the jurist didn't just reject it on the merits; Middlebrooks struggled to contain his disgust with the inanity of the legal complaint.[62]

"These were political grievances masquerading as legal claims," Middlebrooks wrote in his ruling.[63] "This cannot be attributed to incompetent lawyering. It was a deliberate use of the judicial system to pursue a political agenda." He went on to cite the attorneys' "cavalier attitude towards facts," before ultimately sanctioning the former president and his lawyer nearly $1 million for having filed a "frivolous" case.[64]

As Trump hit the comeback trail, his party still appeared preoccupied with replacing the underlying story with a preposterous counternarrative. In June 2023, for example, Republicans on the House Judiciary Committee released a video showing a variety of prominent Democrats talking about Russia trying to help elect Trump in 2016.[65] For the panel's GOP members, each of the featured Democratic claims deserved to be seen as a "lie."

The problem, however, was that each of the featured quotes was entirely accurate,[66] including the most basic claims: Viewers saw Hillary Clinton explain in August 2020, for example, that there was "no question any longer the Russians actively interfered in our election to help Donald Trump. There is no hoax."

This, according to congressional Republicans, had been proven false, creating a bewildering dynamic in which the party was lying about Democrats presenting facts that the GOP preferred to be seen as lies. As Timothy Snyder, a historian at Yale, summarized soon after, "Moscow worked hard to get Trump elected in 2016. Choosing not to know that is choosing not to care about political reality and national security."[67]

The party was unmoved. In August 2023, Senator Marco Rubio published an online message admonishing "the democrat [sic] politicians who falsely claimed Russia hacked the 2016 election."[68] The Florida Republican was in a unique position to know better: Rubio chaired the Senate Intelligence Committee when it released its comprehensive report that helped prove Russia really did launch an intelligence operation targeting the 2016 race by hacking Democratic networks.

Desperate for some kind of political life preserver, partisans on the right clung to the idea that something known as the Durham Report might provide some kind of political relief. When it didn't, the GOP simply pretended otherwise.

After the Justice Department's investigation into the Russia scandal ran its course, and Robert Mueller's findings reached the public, the Trump White House made vague accusations of wrongdoing against federal law enforcement for having launched the probe in the first place. The Justice Department's inspector general conducted a lengthy probe of the investigation, and while Inspector General Michael Horowitz documented instances in which FBI officials were sloppy, he concluded there was nothing improper about the probe.[69]

This, naturally, only outraged the White House further, so Bill Barr tapped a federal prosecutor—U.S. Attorney John Durham—to conduct his own investigation into the investigation. After nearly four years of work, Durham's efforts proved to be largely pointless. By the time he released his final report, the prosecutor had uncovered effectively no new information and made no additional recommendations about possible charges.[70]

Durham did try to prosecute cybersecurity attorney Michael Sussmann, who had tenuous ties to the Clinton campaign, but the case proved to be baseless. Sussmann was acquitted, and after the trial one of the jurors publicly mocked Durham's team for having taken the case to court in the first place.[71]

The lengthy and expensive process—Durham's investigation into the Russia scandal investigation lasted longer than Mueller's original probe of the Russia scandal itself—came to an ignominious end, at which point Republicans found it necessary to play make-believe.

When the Durham Report was released in May 2013, Trump published a series of hysterical missives to his social media platform, suggesting the prosecutor produced evidence of "treason" and "the crime of the century."[72] The former president went on to insist that the Durham Report "spells out in great detail the Democrat [sic] Hoax that was perpetrated upon me and the American people." At 2:15 a.m. local time, apparently still worked up, he added, "THEY ARE SCUM, LIKE COCKROACHES ALL OVER WASHINGTON, D.C."[73]

For those who'd actually read Durham's document, Trump's over-the-top rants were effectively gibberish. Congressional Republicans echoed it anyway. "The Russian hoax was a figment of Hillary Clinton's imagination," Senator Marsha Blackburn of Tennessee declared in a statement.[74] Senator Ted Cruz of Texas condemned reality-based observers for "breathlessly spreading these 'Russia, Russia, Russia' lies."[75] Senator Eric Schmitt pointed to Durham's findings as confirmation that the "collusion" story was a "politically motivated hit job."[76] His fellow Missourian, Senator Josh Hawley, added, "It was all a hoax."[77]

Senator Tommy Tuberville of Alabama told a national television audience, "If people don't go to jail for this, the American people should just stand up and say, 'Listen, enough's enough, let's don't have elections anymore.'"[78]

True to form, conservative media outlets eagerly played along. The front-page headline in the conservative *Washington Times* read, "No Remorse: Democrats Stick to Trump-Russia Collusion Claims Despite Durham Report."[79] Newsmax, a conservative cable outlet, alerted viewers to the developments with an unsubtle on-screen chyron: "Durham Report Proves Russian Collusion Was a Witch Hunt."[80]

The Durham Report did not prove that the scandal was a witch hunt. In fact, Durham made clear in congressional testimony that he barely knew anything about the scandal,[81] and he never even made much of an effort to discredit the underlying controversy. The prosecutor's point was to uncover a supposed "deep state" plot in the Justice Department, but Durham never found anything especially meaningful,[82] and his findings did literally nothing to factually establish GOP conspiracy theories.

Republicans, assuming the public wouldn't actually read the 316-page document, nevertheless felt comfortable presenting an entirely fictional tale about an official report within hours of its release, as if reality had no meaning whatsoever.

A *New York Times* report noted that the GOP's partisan reactions to Durham's findings were "Exhibit A in how the American right seems to be living in its own universe—and how Mr. Trump still dictates the parameters of that separate reality."[83]

The prosecutor had failed spectacularly to discredit the scandal, but Republican officials decided that this accurate story was simply too inconvenient to tolerate, and they were confident they could get away with replacing the truth with a partisan sham.

The party's cynical optimism was rewarded as the propaganda proved incredibly, and predictably, effective with the party's rank-and-file voters. Six months into Trump's term, an ABC News poll found that two-thirds of Republicans rejected the idea that Russia tried to influence the 2016 presidential election.[84] The same data found only 9 percent of GOP voters believed that the president's associates worked cooperatively with the Russian operatives.

In November 2023, a national Quinnipiac University poll asked respondents whether "the Mueller report cleared President Trump of any wrongdoing." A whopping 76 percent of Republican voters said they did, in fact, believe this,[85] despite reality pointing in the opposite direction.

The more evidence emerged that bolstered the scandal, the more Republican officials rewrote the story, and the more their base believed the deceptive tale. By the time Joe Biden was in the Oval Office, there was no longer any doubt in GOP circles that the entirety of the Russia scandal had been exposed as nonsense.

A *Washington Post* analysis explained in June 2023 that Republican voters, taking their cues from party leaders, had bought into the notion that "the whole thing was a hoax, top to bottom."[86] Some GOP partisans weren't confronted with the truth, while others heard facts they preferred to reject.

Either way, the party at every level decided the real story could not stand. The *Post*'s analysis added that for many Republican voters, "the very idea that Russia sought to aid Trump's election is ridiculous. . . . The idea that it was ever worth investigating whether Trump assisted that effort therefore attains a new level of ludicrousness."

Through a campaign of brute-force misinformation, the party had successfully fought a major skirmish in the war on the recent past. Republican leaders told their supporters not to accept the evidence—even the information that had been collected, released, and endorsed by other Republicans—and the party's base was only too pleased to accept the counter-narrative, as if it were real.

In the not-too-distant past, American politics operated under a qualitatively different set of standards. In advance of the 1960 presidential election, as former governor Adlai Stevenson considered another presidential bid, Russian officials reached out to the Illinois Democrat to offer campaign assistance.

Stevenson refused, left the meeting, went home, and documented every detail he could remember. He then went to the authorities, explaining that a foreign adversary had just tried to intervene in an American presidential election.[87]

Russia made similar overtures to Vice President Hubert Humphrey ahead of the 1968 race. The Minnesota Democrat followed Stevenson's example.[88]

Nearly a half century later, one of the lasting consequences of the Trump-Russia scandal was the establishment of an ugly new political standard: this time, when the Kremlin came calling, it found a presidential hopeful who welcomed an outstretched hand from Moscow.

In 2018, Republican representative Dana Rohrabacher insisted "there's not a person in this town" who wouldn't welcome foreign intervention to win an election.[89] A year later, former New York City mayor Rudy Giuliani told a national television audience, "There's nothing wrong with taking information from Russians." The GOP lawyer added that as far as he was concerned, "any candidate" in the United States would gladly "take information" that could be used against a political opponent.[90]

Around the same time, ABC News' George Stephanopoulos asked Trump if his son should've gone to the FBI when he was offered anti-Clinton dirt from Russia. The president said, "Okay, let's put yourself in a position. You're a congressman. Somebody comes up and says, 'Hey, I have information on your opponent. Do you call the FBI? I don't think [so]. . . . You don't call the FBI."[91]

Trump added, "This is somebody that said we have information on your opponent. 'Oh, let me call the FBI.' Give me a break. Life doesn't work that way."

When the anchor reminded the Republican that his own handpicked FBI director said that was exactly how the process should work, Trump replied, "The FBI director is wrong."

Following this to its next logical step, Stephanopoulos asked about the prospect of foreigners offering Trump campaign officials information ahead of the 2020 election. "There's nothing wrong with listening," the incumbent replied. "If somebody called from a country, Norway, 'We have information on your opponent,' oh I think I'd want to hear it."

Asked why he'd want foreign interference in American elections, the president responded, "It's not an interference. They have information, I think I'd take it."

The message to foreign countries couldn't have been clearer: Those abroad hoping to target U.S. elections in order to help Republicans could expect to act with impunity. Not only would some in the party welcome the assistance, they would soon after pretend that the campaign intervention never happened.

There's a reason both of the country's major political parties have traditionally rejected foreign intrusion into U.S. elections: a political system in which international forces compete with American voters is simply untenable. For Trump and others in the GOP to invite foreign actors to help steer our elections for their own purposes strikes at the heart of our national independence—and for them to rewrite the story of such an abuse makes the outrage worse.

CHAPTER 2

"INCREASINGLY DETACHED FROM REALITY"

*Rewriting the Story of the 2020
Presidential Election*

The Berkeley Research Group is largely unknown to most Americans, but in legal and corporate circles, BRG is widely recognized as a leading consulting firm with an impressive roster of prominent clients. With this in mind, when Donald Trump's political operation, reluctant to accept the results of the 2020 presidential election, set out to discredit the outcome, it hired BRG researchers to lend a hand.

The outgoing president and his team commissioned the firm in December 2020 to uncover evidence that would bolster Republican conspiracy theories related to the incumbent's defeat, and the remit was effectively limitless: The Berkeley Research Group would go through the election results with a fine-tooth comb, looking for evidence of voter fraud and election irregularities. If there were problems with voting machines, BRG researchers would find them. If ballots were cast in the name of dead voters, BRG researchers would uncover them, too.

Once the firm's work was complete, BRG would compile its findings into a report, which Team Trump could then share, in part or in whole, with the rest of the world.

That is, so long as Republicans liked what the firm's researchers had to say.

As it turned out, the former president and his aides kept the Berkeley Research Group's findings under wraps for the most predictable of reasons: The firm determined that Trump's conspiracy theories had no basis in reality. After carefully scrutinizing the election, BRG concluded that Joe Biden was the rightful winner.[1]

The *Washington Post* spoke to an insider familiar with the results of BRG's research. "They looked at everything: change of addresses, illegal immigrants, ballot harvesting, people voting twice, machines being tampered with, ballots that were sent to vacant addresses that were returned and voted. Literally anything you could think of," the source explained. "Voter turnout anomalies, date of birth anomalies, whether dead people voted. If there was anything under the sun that could be thought of, they looked at it."[2]

Trump's political operation, in other words, spent $600,000 on a research project that concluded, in no uncertain terms, that everything the former president said about his defeat was untrue. The Berkeley Research Group could provide extensive information to its client, but it couldn't tell him that he'd been cheated out of a victory—because that was not what happened.

It was not the only contract of its kind. Team Trump spent $750,000 on a parallel research project with Simpatico Software Systems, a tech company that was also tasked with scrutinizing a series of GOP conspiracy theories related to the 2020 race. The results were identical.[3]

Ken Block, the firm's founder, concluded, "Every fraud claim I was asked to investigate was false."

This was no doubt discouraging for Trump and his staff. In the immediate aftermath of his election defeat, the Republican rejected the legitimacy of the vote totals and started peddling self-serving lies that he desperately wanted to be true. To that end, he wrote sizable checks to some of the industry's top private-sector researchers, who had an incentive to satisfy their powerful client's wishes. Trump hoped they'd come up with something, *anything*, that might help bolster the conclusions he'd already drawn.

The firms could not, however, present evidence that didn't exist.

What's more, the researchers weren't the only ones presenting Trump with inconvenient electoral truths. The Republican's campaign manager told him he lost, and that his fraud claims were wrong.[4] Trump's lawyers told him the same thing.[5] So did his campaign data experts.[6] And Justice Department officials.[7] And Department of Homeland Security officials.[8]

As former attorney general William Barr—yet another insider who also told Trump the truth about his defeat[9]—later explained under oath during testimony to congressional investigators, "There was never an indication of interest in what the actual facts were."[10]

It was at that point that the defeated president, his party, and its voting base had a responsibility to grudgingly come to terms with the will of the voters and move on. They instead did what the party too often does in response to crushing developments it struggled to explain away: they rewrote the story.

What made this propaganda campaign different from most, however, was the tactical timeline. Before Republicans could rewrite the history of the 2020 race, they felt the need to *pre*-write it.

In June 2020, Trump was trailing in the polls and struggling with an underwhelming approval rating. It was a dynamic that led him to start laying the rhetorical groundwork in anticipation of a defeat he intended to discredit. "This will be, in my opinion, the most corrupt election in the history of our country," the incumbent told an audience in Arizona.[11]

There was no historical parallel for a sitting American president making such an overt effort—based on literally no evidence—to undermine public confidence in his own country's electoral system. It was also a sign of things to come.

A month later, during a Fox News interview, a network anchor asked for a "direct answer" as to whether Trump would accept the results of the election. "I have to see," the Republican replied,[12] leaving open a door that responsible leaders are supposed to keep closed.

The president wasn't the only prominent voice in his party taking indefensible steps to discourage Americans from trusting their elections process. Bill Barr delivered congressional testimony in July 2020, insisting that it was "common sense" to believe foreign adversaries were positioned to successfully sway U.S. elections with counterfeit ballots.[13]

As the nation's chief law enforcement official really ought to have known, his testimony was plainly wrong: U.S. intelligence agencies and state election officials from both parties were quick to explain[14] that there were all kinds of safeguards in place—including tracking bar codes and envelopes that require voter signatures—that made Barr's scenario "virtually impossible."[15] In fact, long before the 2020 race, several states—some "red," some "blue"—conducted elections by mail without incident.

The attorney general nevertheless kept the offensive going, telling the *Chicago Tribune* that nefarious fraudsters were well positioned to "pay off a postman" with bribes in order to illegally obtain mail-in ballots.[16] University of Kentucky law professor Josh Douglas, an election law expert, described Barr's rhetoric as "wild, fanciful, and completely false lies," adding, "This is beyond unprofessional."[17]

But as Election Day neared, it was Trump who went to the most hysterical lengths to establish a narrative he could lean on in the event of his likely defeat. A *Washington Post* fact-check piece published in September 2020—as early voting began in some parts of the country—highlighted a series of outlandish election-related claims from the president, and concluded, "This is a breathtaking onslaught on the truth and the integrity of an upcoming U.S. election. We expect it from Russia, especially after the copious evidence of its disinformation campaign in 2016 to benefit Trump. But to see it emanate from the president of the United States [and his partisan allies] is nothing short of stunning."[18]

Days later, Dan Coats, Trump's former director of national intelligence, wrote an op-ed reminding the public that the United States' enemies abroad "want us to concede in advance that our voting systems are faulty or fraudulent."[19] The Indiana Republican's caution went unheeded by his former boss, who furiously told the electorate that the 2020 race was "rigged"[20] as part of a dangerous crusade to delegitimize the process.

On November 1, 2020, two days before Election Day, there were reports that the president was prepared to declare victory on Election Night, no matter what the results showed.[21] It was against that backdrop that Trump entered the White House's East Room at 2:21 a.m. the morning of November 4, and told a group of supporters that the election was being taken from him. "As far as I am concerned," he declared, "we already have won it."[22]

In the same remarks, Trump equated counting votes with perpetrating a "fraud."[23] Moments later, he suggested vote-counting should continue, but only in states where he was trailing.[24] Americans had simply never seen a sitting president launch such an assault on his own country's system of elections.

A day later, the Republican read from a prepared text, lied to the public about the vote tallies, and effectively pleaded with voters not to trust the U.S. electoral system[25]—not because he'd uncovered systemic flaws, but because the system presented him with election results he didn't like.

It was less of a tantrum and more of a calculated attack. Writing for Vox, Ezra Klein explained, "What we're seeing is the sitting President of the United States using the power of his office, his megaphone, and his supporters, to try to stop the votes against him from being counted. Not a drill, a joke, a hypothetical. It's happening."[26]

A day later, Kevin McCarthy, the GOP's House leader, appeared on Fox News and similarly declared, "President Trump won this election. . . . Republicans will not be silenced."[27] Senator Lindsey Graham appeared on the same party-aligned network and was asked whether GOP legislators in key states should consider invalidating the local results and awarding their electoral votes to the losing candidate. "Everything should be on the table," the South Carolinian said.[28]

In the days and weeks that followed, the more the Republican Party was bombarded by reality, the more its officials clung to a counternarrative in which the 2020 race was corrupted by systemic fraud. Trump urged the GOP to join him in his alternate reality, and officials en masse accepted the invitation.[29]

"We don't yet have any evidence proving voter fraud was committed in this election," *Politico*'s Tim Alberta wrote in the race's immediate aftermath.[30] "We do have evidence that Republicans—from the president to congressional leaders to the party chair and her aides—are lying to the public."

Alberta added, "After four years of turning a blind eye to the president's subversive rhetoric and manic behavior and relentless dishonesty, the ultimate test for the Republican Party was whether it would accommodate the president's rebellion against this country's democratic norms or denounce it. The Republican Party has failed that test. . . . A healthy Republican Party would not abide this. . . . In November 2016, Republicans looked upon Trump's victory and wondered if there was any going back. In November 2020, they looked upon Trump's defeat and decided the answer was no."[31]

After the race was called for the Democratic ticket, and the White House made clear it had no interest in a peaceful transition of power, Senator Chris Murphy delivered memorable remarks on the chamber floor. "My colleagues," the Connecticut Democrat said, "there is an epidemic of delusion that is spreading out from the White House and infecting the entire Republican party in the wake of this election."[32]

Michael Abramowitz, the president of Freedom House, a nonprofit group that monitors international democratic movements, could hardly believe his eyes. "I never would have imagined seeing something like this in America," he said.[33]

Abramowitz added that even if Trump ultimately failed to overturn his defeat, "by convincing a large part of the population that there was widespread fraud, he is seeding a myth that could endure for years."

It wasn't long before the party's bad-faith arguments started colliding with one another. While the defeated president was outraged by the voters' verdict, plenty of other GOP candidates fared quite well in the 2020 elections, to the delight of party officials.

The result, however, was a partisan conundrum: on the one hand, Republicans asked the public to believe the election cycle had been corrupted by widespread fraud, and the results were not to be trusted. On the other hand, those same Republicans also asked the public to join in the celebration of election results the party actually liked.

The *New York Times*' Tom Edsall explained that the party-imposed drama came amidst an election cycle "in which Republican victories up and down the ballot are accepted unquestioningly, while votes for president-elect Biden *on the same ballots* are not."[34]

The party responded to the contradiction by ignoring it. Indeed, there was no longer any question as to whether Republicans were being consistent, principled, or honest. They obviously were not. But GOP officials didn't care about having been caught. They felt no shame. There was no embarrassment. There was only a cynical assumption that much of the country would disregard the unfolding facts and be fooled into believing their propaganda—just so long as Americans didn't look too closely at the details.

At times, watching Team Trump condemn the election and its results was like watching a severely intoxicated person try to walk a straight line. In the aftermath of Biden's victory, members of the Republican operation struggled to decide whether they wanted vote counts to continue or stop. They heralded some parts of ballots while rejecting others. They both believed and disbelieved news organizations that called elections.

They threw around affidavits related to conspiracy theories that might as well have been written in crayon.[35] They concocted weird allegations, then scrambled to find evidence that might substantiate them, and then asked for patience when they discovered no such evidence existed.[36] The party had months to prepare for this eventuality, and it quickly became obvious that the time was not well spent.

Most have heard the expression about throwing stuff against a wall to see what sticks, but in this case, the president and his allies struggled to find stuff, and they were even less sure where the wall was.

———

Undaunted, the radical crusade continued. In early December 2020, Trump-aligned Texas attorney general Ken Paxton filed suit against four battleground states—Georgia, Michigan, Pennsylvania, and Wisconsin—whose election results helped deliver the White House to Biden. As part of the litigation, the Texas Republican, who led "Lawyers for Trump," asked the U.S. Supreme Court to block the states from voting in the electoral college.[37]

Reuters' Brad Heath explained that Paxton was "literally asking the Supreme Court to throw out the results of other states' presidential elections, set aside the millions of votes cast in states that are not Texas, and have other state legislatures make Trump president. This is, to be clear, a lawsuit filed in the Supreme Court making some of the same specious, patently false claims that have been filed—and rejected—by other people trying to have the courts make Trump president again. Only this one was filed by an arm of state government."[38]

Legal experts wasted little time in describing the lawsuit as "bonkers."[39] MSNBC's Chris Hayes added that Paxton's case was "both laughably buffoonish and just unspeakably poisonous in what it represents."[40]

The justices ultimately discarded the litigation,[41] adding to a lengthy list of failed legal challenges to the 2020 results, but not before the case was endorsed by Trump, seventeen Republican state attorneys general, and nearly two-thirds of the Republicans in the U.S. House[42]—including future speaker Kevin McCarthy and his successor, Mike Johnson. The Atlantic's David Graham wrote that these GOP officials had gone from "coddling a sore loser to effectively abandoning democracy."[43]

Around the same time, Trump's legal team, led by Rudy Giuliani, held a bewildering press conference at the Republican National Committee, presenting a cartoonish tale of imagined voter fraud, corrupted voting machines, scary foreign philanthropists, "communist money," the Clinton Foundation, a loose band of antifascist activists called Antifa, Cuba, and possibly China.[44] As part of the same odd laundry list, the public was also asked to believe the anti-Trump election plot had something to do with Hugo Chavez, the Venezuelan president who'd been dead for seven years.

Christopher Krebs, who led the Department of Homeland Security's Cybersecurity and Infrastructure Security Agency before Trump fired him for telling the truth about the election,[45] described the press conference as "the most dangerous 1 hour and 45 minutes of television in American history. And possibly the craziest."[46]

The defeated president was undeterred, telling Americans on a nearly daily basis that he not only won the race he lost, but that he prevailed by a "tremendous amount."[47] In early December 2020, Trump released a forty-six-minute video on Facebook, recorded in the White House's Diplomatic Reception Room, in which he packaged together practically every election-related lie he could think of.

While Trump described it as perhaps "the most important speech" he'd ever delivered, the Associated Press reported that the Republican was "increasingly detached from reality . . . unspooling one misstatement after another."[48]

When members of the electoral college met to make Biden's

victory official, Trump told Fox News "we caught them" engaging in election fraud[49]—in context, it was far from clear who "we" and "them" referred to—before turning to social media to declare, "I WON THE ELECTION IN A LANDSLIDE!"[50]

The truth was easy to believe: a scandal-plagued incumbent with a thin record ran for reelection while failing spectacularly to deal with a dangerous public health emergency. He ran against a respected and well-known rival whom voters saw as experienced and mainstream. Polls showed the challenger well positioned to prevail, and the election results were entirely in line with widely held expectations.

But that clearly wasn't good enough for the GOP. On the contrary, the nature of the rewrite effort came into focus rather quickly: Republicans would replace an accurate story with a fictional one by repeating a baseless lie, adding exclamation points, throwing around scary-sounding phrases such as "suitcases full of ballots" and "ballot dumps," and waiting for party members and their allies to nod their heads in agreement.

The outgoing president was not without opportunities to substantiate his rhetoric. At a campaign event in Georgia held a month after his defeat, Trump assured his followers, "We have so much evidence. They say, 'Oh, he doesn't have the evidence.' We have so much evidence, we don't know what to do with it."[51]

In the months and years that followed, the Republican and his aides chose not to share any of that evidence for reasons they struggled to explain. In June 2022, for example, a year and a half after Biden's inauguration, Team Trump issued a twelve-page report that it claimed offered proof of election "cheating." In reality, the document was an embarrassing rehash of absurdities the Republican had already peddled.[52]

A *Washington Post* analysis characterized it as "something of a greatest-hits collection for [Trump's] long-standing crusade against reality. . . . Even now, 19 months after the election, he demonstrates no ability to discern fact from fiction about the election results but also shows no interest in trying to draw such a distinction."[53]

More than a year later, in August 2023, Trump announced in a written statement that he was poised to hold a press conference to unveil a "Large, Complex, Detailed but Irrefutable REPORT on the Presidential Election Fraud" in 2020, most notably in Georgia.[54] The Republican's operation had reportedly worked on the document "for many weeks" and aides leaked word that it was "more than 100 pages" long.[55]

Trump soon after canceled the presentation and said the report would not be released after all.[56] Its contents, the former president assured supporters, would instead eventually be shared in court. (Trump's lawyers had privately advised him that holding a press conference in which he promoted election lies would "complicate his legal problems."[57])

Those who'd been waiting for years for "irrefutable" proof of election irregularities would have to go without.

The former president occasionally used his social media platform to suggest that in his rewritten story of the 2020 election, there was one chapter that he was especially eager for the public to take seriously. It was called *2000 Mules*.

At issue was a documentary film, directed by a prominent far-right provocateur named Dinesh D'Souza. The project purported to have "smoking gun" evidence of systemic fraud thanks to geolocation tracking data, which, according to the film's creators, showed thousands of Americans making suspicious stops at mail-in vote drop boxes.[58]

Independent analyses were unimpressed by the findings. The *New York Times* characterized the movie as "a Big Lie in a New Package," noting that even some on the right expressed discomfort with the project and its conclusions.[59] Similarly, the Associated Press said the film was burdened by "gaping holes"[60]; *Washington Post* analyses characterized its findings as "dishonest"[61] and "misleading"[62]; while the Daily Beast concluded that the movie was "stupid."[63]

Writing for The Bulwark, a prominent online outlet for political commentary, Amanda Carpenter described *2000 Mules* as unintentionally "hilarious," adding that the documentary was a "tour de force exploring the limits of how many suckers there are willing to pay for fantasy."[64]

She wasn't the only one who was amused by the project's unpersuasive pitch. When Congress' bipartisan January 6 committee asked Bill Barr for his reactions to the film's findings, the former attorney general literally laughed at the movie and its claims.[65]

"If you take 2 million cell phones and figure out where they are physically in a big city like Atlanta or wherever, just by definition, you're going to find any hundreds of them have passed by and spend time in the vicinity of these boxes," he testified. The Republican lawyer went on to tell federal investigators, "The premise that if you go by a box, five boxes or whatever it was, you know that that's 'a mule' is just indefensible."[66]

Trump not only endorsed the documentary, he also arranged a screening at Mar-a-Lago.[67] The film was similarly embraced with great enthusiasm by a variety of congressional Republicans—in the House[68] and Senate[69]—including prominent election deniers such as Reps. Matt Gaetz and Marjorie Taylor Greene.[70]

In the Republicans' war on the recent past, there was nothing mysterious about the motivation behind the party's propaganda campaign against the 2020 election. Trump, unwilling to accept the fact that the American electorate had rejected him by a margin of more than 7 million popular votes and 74 electoral votes, concocted a dangerous tale about voter fraud he couldn't prove, schemers he couldn't identify, and corruption he couldn't find.

In early June 2020, the incumbent said about a possible defeat, "Certainly, if I don't win, I don't win." He added that if he ultimately came up short, "you go on, do other things."[71]

Trump didn't mean a word of it. He spent the months leading up to Election Day 2020 preparing to reject the legitimacy of a possible loss; he spent the aftermath of the election lying about and trying to reverse the outcome; and he spent the ensuing months and years pretending that he'd secretly won the race that forced him from the White House.

The preferred counternarrative was clear: Americans were supposed to believe either that Trump's reelection bid was victorious or that Biden's win was inherently suspect, made possible only by corruption.

The misinformation battle was joined by GOP lawmakers in Congress—two-thirds of whom voted against certifying the 2020 election results[72]—and allied media outlets. Indeed, a defamation lawsuit filed by Dominion Voting Systems against Fox News generated devastating information about the cable outlet: the civil case filed by the voting machine company produced evidence that suggested Fox promoted bogus pro-Trump election claims it knew to be false, on purpose, in order to placate its audience and protect its stock price, market share, and business model.[73]

But when assessing the broader campaign, no contingent was more important than the propaganda's intended target: the Republican Party's base of supporters.

Confronted by an endless stream of lies and tweets, fundraising appeals and conspiracy theories, rallies and cable-news segments, the GOP's rank-and-file members were subjected to a relentless messaging barrage in service of a single goal: the story they heard from independent sources of information needed to be supplanted by a rewritten story Republican officials preferred.

The whitewashing worked like a charm.

In November 2020, roughly two weeks after the Democratic ticket's victory, a national poll from Monmouth University asked respondents, "Do you believe Joe Biden won this election fair and square, or do you believe that he only won it due to voter fraud?" A 60 percent majority of Americans overall saw Biden as the legitimate victor, but 70 percent of Republican voters—and 77 percent of Trump voters—believed the opposite.[74]

Many observers suggested at the time that results like

these needed to be taken with a grain of salt. The GOP base was surprised by the outcome—Republicans had been led to believe Trump's success was inevitable—and the expectation was that surveys conducted in the immediate aftermath of the election reflected red-hot emotional reactions more than sincere attitudes.

In time, the disbelief and anger would fade; Trump would fail to produce evidence; policymakers' attention would shift toward governing; and even the most head-in-the-sand partisans would recognize the merits of moving on.

At least, that was the idea, which soon proved naïve. In the months and years that followed, as the GOP at the institutional level continued to pretend that the 2020 race had been "rigged," Republican voters took cues from their party seriously and clung to the delusion that came to be known as Trump's "Big Lie."

By the summer of 2023, CNN released the findings of a national survey about the legitimacy of Biden's presidency. The results were nearly identical to the data from November 2020: 69 percent of Republicans said the Democrat was not the rightful winner of the last presidential election, reality be damned.[75]

More than one thousand days after the former president's defeat, more than two-thirds of his party was still more inclined to believe the rewritten story than the truth, which in turn helped position Trump as the front-runner for his party's 2024 nomination. For many GOP voters, the calculus was simple: if Trump had already won twice, why abandon the candidate with a proven track record of success?

The party's voters had been told not to trust election

results. Or election administrators. Or election lawyers. Or independent news organizations. Or political scientists. Or the courts. They were instead told to put their faith in easily discredited nonsense from a failed and corrupt former president, his conspiratorial allies, and conservative media outlets that profited from his propaganda.

And so, they did.

In many instances, GOP officials put the polling results to pernicious use. In early January 2021, for example, just four days before the attack on the U.S. Capitol, eleven Senate Republicans, led by Texas's Ted Cruz, announced plans to object when the chamber certified the election results. The far-right contingent defended its gambit by pointing to surveys showing public "distrust" in the vote tallies.[76]

It gradually became one of the party's favorite talking points. Before stepping down as chairman of the Senate Homeland Security Committee, Senator Ron Johnson announced plans to hold investigatory hearings into election "irregularities"[77]—not because the Wisconsin Republican had uncovered wrongdoing, but because he'd seen polls that showed "a large percentage of the American public" rejecting the legitimacy of the 2020 results.

The result was a vicious circle: GOP officials lied about the election, which led the party's base to accept the conspiracy theories as true. Republicans would then argue that their bogus claims had merit by pointing to the public-opinion data, which only encouraged GOP officials to lie some more, starting the process anew.

In other words, Republicans in positions of authority tried to justify their misinformation by referencing polls that showed people being fooled by their misinformation. But a con man's scam doesn't become less crooked based on his number of victims.

The *New Yorker*'s Susan Glasser noted in response to the polling data, "This is a big red flashing light of trouble for American democracy."[78] The assessment was true on multiple fronts.

First, in the wake of Trump's defeat, GOP policymakers at the state level scrambled to impose new post-2020 voting restrictions, claiming that they would improve public confidence in elections systems—confidence that had been shaken by those same GOP policymakers and their discredited conspiracy theories.

The Brennan Center for Justice at the New York University School of Law found that in 2021 alone, nineteen states approved thirty-three laws that made it harder for Americans to participate in their own democracy, effectively weaponizing the party's "Big Lie."[79]

Second, in several Republican-led states, officials didn't just create new barriers to make voting more difficult, they also created "voter fraud units" and "election integrity units" composed of investigators who were tasked with focusing exclusively on election-related crimes.

These expensive law enforcement endeavors, predictably, proved to be wildly unnecessary. An Associated Press investigation concluded that the units "provided no indication of systemic problems" with voting systems anywhere, which was "just what election experts had expected."[80] Taxpayers were nevertheless on the hook for these boondoggles, which in some states, intimidated voters without cause.[81]

Third, evidence emerged of the GOP adopting a radical new normal in which accepting unfavorable election outcomes became optional. Shortly before the 2022 midterm cycle, for example, Wisconsin's Ron Johnson was asked whether he'd honor the results in his reelection bid—a question that journalists didn't think to ask in the United States before the Trump era.

"We'll see what happens," the GOP senator replied, questioning whether Democratic rascals might "have something up their sleeves."[82]

He had a disheartening amount of company. In September 2022, the *Washington Post* published a report on a dozen Republican candidates in competitive gubernatorial and Senate races, each of whom declined to say whether they would accept the legitimacy of the upcoming results.[83] The *New York Times* conducted a similar endeavor, asking statewide nominees in midterm battlegrounds whether they would commit to accepting the elections' outcomes. The results were similar: most Republicans either wouldn't answer or wouldn't make such a commitment, while Democratic candidates said they would respect the results, win or lose.[84]

The *Times*' David Leonhardt, reviewing burgeoning threats to our democracy, explained, "The first threat is acute: a growing movement inside one of the country's two major parties—the Republican Party—to refuse to accept defeat in an election."[85] That refusal was driven in large part by the story the GOP had told itself about the 2020 race.

Finally, there were genuine security risks to consider. In June 2021, for example, Reuters ran a striking report on the "barrage of threats and intimidation against election officials and their families" coming from those who accepted Trump's counternarratives about the 2020 race as accurate.[86]

Much of the report quoted hair-raising threats against prominent election officials who'd infuriated the right for one reason or another, but Reuters added that "many others whose lives have been threatened were low- or mid-level workers, just doing their jobs."

In the months that followed, officials at the Department of Homeland Security repeatedly issued warnings to law enforcement about "heightened threat environments" caused by "widespread online proliferation of false or misleading narratives regarding unsubstantiated widespread election fraud."[87]

Or put another way, too many extremists had come to believe too many election lies, and the result was too many real-world threats. Indeed, January 6 was itself an example of the phenomenon: radicalized Trump followers, fueled by falsehoods, were led to believe their democracy was being subverted, leaving them to conclude that an insurrectionist riot was justified.

In a healthy, functioning democracy, citizens recognize the legitimacy of elections as the sole vehicle for setting the nation's direction. The more that Republican voters were led to believe that vote totals were shams, the more dangerous the circumstances became.

On the first anniversary of the January 6 attack, Biden delivered remarks in which he reminded Americans, "You can't love your country only when you win."[88]

The Democrat added, "At this moment, we must decide: What kind of nation are we going to be? Are we going to be a nation that accepts political violence as a norm? Are we going to be a nation where we allow partisan election officials to overturn the legally expressed will of the people? Are we going to be a nation that lives not by the light of the truth but in the shadow of lies?"

Those need not be rhetorical questions. As dramatic as the post-2020-election crisis was, and as important as the lingering consequences have been, this watershed moment crystalized a foundational challenge for the electorate: either Americans will resolve their differences at the ballot box or they won't. For far too much of the Republican Party, the answer comes with a qualifier: election results are to be embraced when GOP candidates prevail.

To borrow a line from Shakespeare's *King Lear*, that way madness lies.

CHAPTER 3

"A NORMAL TOURIST VISIT"

Rewriting the Story of the January 6
Attack on the U.S. Capitol

When looking for major events in modern American history that would be easy to whitewash, the January 6 attack on the U.S. Capitol would appear to be near the bottom of the list. The riot was simply too well understood to be recharacterized as anything other than what it was: insurrectionist violence, fueled by partisan lies, targeting the American seat of government for the purposes of helping a defeated presidential candidate claim illegitimate power.

The indelible video and images were simply too powerful to ignore or forget. The rioters on the Senate floor. The guns drawn at the entry to the House chamber. The noose displayed on a gallows. The "hang Mike Pence" chants. The plastic zip-tie handcuffs. The elected officials running to safety. The Confederate flag that never reached Capitol Hill during the Civil War, but which was carried down congressional hallways in

January 2021. A rioter grinning with apparent pride as he put his foot on the speaker of the House's desk. The insurrectionists breaking into the building, climbing its walls, violently clashing with law enforcement, all while Trump flags waved around them.

Just as important, there were no ambiguities surrounding Donald Trump, his public pleas for his supporters to join him in the nation's capital, or the preriot remarks he delivered to a group of radicalized followers at the Ellipse, against the backdrop of the White House. "You'll never take back our country with weakness," the president declared.[1] "You have to show strength and you have to be strong. We have come to demand that Congress do the right thing and only count the electors who have been lawfully slated."

As Congress prepared to certify the election results, and the Republican deployed his acolytes, he added, "We fight. We fight like hell. And if you don't fight like hell, you're not going to have a country anymore."

Trump went on to tell his enraged disciples, "Our country has had enough. . . . We will stop the steal. . . . You will have an illegitimate president. That is what you will have, and we can't let that happen." While peddling lies and hoaxes, the president concluded, "We will not be intimidated into accepting the hoaxes and the lies that we've been forced to believe over the past several weeks."[2]

The chilling footage was seen by too many people, domestically and around the world, for reality to yield. The details surrounding the attack—from its perpetrators to its instigators, its purpose to its effects, its organizers to its victims—were too well documented by investigators, policymakers, journalists, and prosecutors.

The idea of a political party even *attempting* to rewrite the story of the assault seemed plainly ridiculous. It would not happen. It could not happen.

That is, until Republicans decided it had to happen.

Within hours of the Capitol being cleared, Representative Paul Gosar of Arizona turned to social media to suggest the attack was an example of "leftist violence."[3] Soon after, Representative Matt Gaetz of Florida appeared on the House floor and declared his belief that the violence could be attributed to "Antifa" members who were "masquerading as Trump supporters."[4]

Former half-term Alaska governor Sarah Palin, citing "pictures" she claimed to have seen, insisted that "a lot" of the violence was committed by "the Antifa folks."[5] Representative Mo Brooks was slightly more circumspect when speaking to Fox Business's Lou Dobbs the night of the riot, but the Alabama Republican nevertheless told the national television audience that there was "some indication that fascist Antifa elements were involved."[6]

Fox News' Laura Ingraham spent much of her hour-long January 6 program claiming that there were pro-Trump protesters at the Capitol, but their ranks had been infiltrated by left-wing extremists.[7] To bolster her assertions, the host pointed to nothing in particular.

A week after the violence, 222 House Democrats were joined by ten House Republicans in impeaching Trump for a second time, charging the president with "incitement of insurrection" for his role in the attack. When the case went to the upper chamber for an impeachment trial, the defendant's legal team struggled to present a coherent defense, though they were careful to tell senators that Antifa deserved at least part of the blame for the assault on the Capitol.[8] (Seven GOP senators soon after joined with fifty Democrats in voting to convict Trump. The fifty-seven members constituted a majority, but not the two-thirds majority needed for a conviction.)

Around the same time, Senator Ron Johnson—labeled the Republican Party's "foremost amplifier of conspiracy theories and disinformation" by the *New York Times*[9]—participated in the Senate's first-ever hearing on the attack. The Wisconsin lawmaker decided to use his time with the microphone to read an item from a right-wing blog, which claimed that "fake Trump protesters" were behind the assault.[10]

Around the same time, Mike Shirkey, the highest ranking Republican elected official in Michigan, joined the parade, declaring in reference to January 6, "That wasn't Trump people. That's been a hoax from day one. . . . It was all staged."[11]

It was not all staged. In fact, Christopher Wray, the Trump-appointed FBI director, appeared before the Senate Judiciary Committee in early March 2021 and testified that federal investigators could find no evidence of "anarchist violent extremists or people subscribing to Antifa in connection with the 6th."[12]

The GOP base had nevertheless heard the misinformation—and despite the obvious absurdities, a striking number of rank-and-file Republican voters believed what they were told to believe. A national poll conducted by *USA Today* and Suffolk University in mid-February 2021 found that 58 percent of Trump voters embraced the idea that January 6 violence was "mostly an Antifa-inspired attack that only involved a few Trump supporters."[13]

These Republicans, like everyone else, saw what transpired on Capitol Hill, but they found it easier to believe a head-spinning counternarrative—a loose alliance of far-left antifascist groups pretended to be right-wing activists, as part of an elaborate ruse—instead of the truth.

In time, the idea that the left was somehow responsible for pro-Trump violence proved unsustainable, even for the most rabid conspiracy theorists. It was at that point that prominent GOP voices decided to concoct a new story, which was largely the opposite of their original tale: instead of far-left criminals being responsible for a historic attack, many Republicans concluded, it was actually conservative patriots who, in this newly revised story, were being persecuted for little more than raising concerns about election integrity.

The principal author of the counternarrative was, of course, Trump himself.

During the attack on the Capitol, the incumbent president sat on his hands and ignored calls to intervene. He'd helped incite a riot, and he had little interest in calming the gang he'd summoned for this very purpose. Hours after the violence in his name began, after receiving desperate and impassioned pleas from GOP allies, Trump grudgingly released a video to social media urging his mob of followers to disperse.

But even then, the Republican made clear that he sympathized with the rioters and saw them as partners. In the online clip, Trump continued to lie to his supporters, claiming there'd been "an election that was stolen from us." He added, "We love you. You're very special."[14]

It was soon after when the outgoing president came to terms with the fact that his position was politically unten-able. Not only was the public revulsion to the violence too fierce to disregard, but members of the White House Cabinet initiated quiet conversations about removing Trump from office by way of the Twenty-Fifth Amendment.[15] He and his team scrambled to find political "cover"[16] in order to ensure that he'd be able to complete the final two weeks of his term.

As a consequence, Trump became a January 6 critic—at least temporarily. "Like all Americans, I am outraged by the violence, lawlessness and mayhem," the Republican said on January 7, describing the events from a day earlier as a "hei-nous attack."[17] Reading from a prepared text, Trump added, "The demonstrators who infiltrated the Capitol have defiled the seat of American democracy. . . . To those who engage in the acts of violence and destruction: You do not represent our country, and to those who broke the law: You will pay."

Five days later, the president condemned the "mob" that "stormed the Capitol and trashed the halls of government." On the final full day of his term, again reading from a writ-ten script, Trump added, "All Americans were horrified by the assault on our Capitol. Political violence is an attack on every-thing we cherish as Americans. It can never be tolerated."[18]

Once out of office, however, his interest in maintaining the pretense waned. In March 2021, nine weeks after his departure from the White House, Trump appeared on Fox News and said that while some of his supporters went a little too far inside the Capitol, they posed "zero threat" to anyone.[19] He added the rioters were merely "hugging and kissing the police and the guards," before suggesting there was a "great relationship" between law enforcement and members of the mob.

The revisionist history was breathtaking, even by contemporary GOP standards. The threats posed by those perpetrating the attack were obvious: armed extremists didn't just try to halt congressional certification of the 2020 election, they also hunted for Trump's perceived political foes while chanting violent threats.

What's more, these same rioters violently clashed with law enforcement, and an estimate from the head of the Capitol Police officers' union indicated that roughly 140 officers were injured as part of the attack.[20] Among them was Officer Michael Fanone, who was grabbed and dragged into a mob by a man who boasted, "I got one!" At that point, pro-Trump rioters tased the officer, took his badge and radio, and threatened to murder him with his own gun.[21]

Fanone was neither hugged nor kissed by his assailants.

Five police officers who had served at the Capitol on January 6 subsequently died, including Capitol Police officer Brian Sicknick, who was attacked by the president's supporters. Four of the five took their own lives.[22]

For the former president, however, this was just the start of an expansive rewrite campaign. Within days of his bizarre "zero threat" comments, Trump described the rioters as members of "a loving crowd."[23] By July 2021, the Republican said those charged with crimes related to the attack were being treated "unbelievably unfairly,"[24] though he pointed to no examples of unfair treatment.

Four days later, reflecting on those who attended his "Stop the Steal" rally before he deployed them to Capitol Hill, Trump described them as "peaceful people," adding, "The love—the love in the air, I have never seen anything like it." The former president went on to celebrate what he described as "a lovefest between the police, the Capitol Police, and the people that walked down to the Capitol."[25]

Trump's support for suspected and convicted January 6 criminals grew even more explicit in the months and years that followed. The Republican's initial rhetoric about his opposition to "lawlessness and mayhem" and his disdain for those who "defiled the seat of American democracy" by participating in a "heinous" attack were replaced by gushing praise. In September 2021, for example, the former president issued a written statement that read in part, "Our hearts and minds are with the people being persecuted so unfairly relating to the January 6th protest concerning the Rigged Presidential Election."[26]

A month later, he insisted that "the real insurrection" was the election itself,[27] not the Capitol assault.

By February 2022, Trump was comfortable describing January 6 criminals as "patriots."[28] Four months later, he used his social media platform to argue that the riot "represented the greatest movement in the history of our Country."[29] Also in June 2022, the Republican said that if voters returned him to power, he'd "very, very seriously" consider presidential pardons for convicted rioters, adding, "very, very seriously."[30]

In September 2022, Trump raised the prospect of some kind of official government "apology" for January 6 convicts.

In the same set of remarks, the former president said he'd extend financial support to the families of rioters.[31]

But to fully appreciate the scope of the party's willingness to wage war on the recent past, it's important to see Trump's deceptions as part of a larger partisan campaign. In March 2021, for example, barely two months after the Capitol Hill assault, Ron Johnson abandoned his "fake Trump protesters" talking point and instead argued that those who attacked the Capitol "truly respect law enforcement" and deserved to be seen as people who "loved this country."[32]

By mid-May, roughly four months after insurrectionists stormed Capitol Hill, the House Oversight Committee held a hearing on the violence, and some of its GOP members broke new and audacious ground. Arizona's Paul Gosar, for example, slammed the Justice Department for "harassing" suspected rioters, whom he described as "peaceful patriots."[33]

Georgia's Andrew Clyde applauded Trump's rabid mob for having behaved "in an orderly fashion."[34] The congressman went on to say, "If you didn't know that TV footage was a video from January the 6th, you would actually think it was a normal tourist visit."[35] (A couple of months later, during another House hearing, Clyde was offered an opportunity to walk back his comments. He refused. In reference to the "normal tourist visit" comments, the Republican said, "I stand by that exact statement as I said it."[36])

The public had already seen what happened. In the propagandistic rewrite, Americans were expected to believe that the rioters were victims, worthy not only of public support but also pity.

Former defense secretary William Cohen, who was also a longtime GOP member of Congress, was among the many who were gobsmacked. "Those members who are trying to say, 'No big deal on Jan. 6,' they're trying to perform a frontal lobotomy on the American people, a side effect which is mental dullness," the retired Maine Republican said.[37]

Around the same time, Republican representative Adam Kinzinger added, "When I saw my colleagues speak, you know, it feels like it's in *1984*—something you see out of North Korea, where it's like, 'We're just going to state whatever we want the reality to be.'"[38]

Kinzinger, who served on the bipartisan congressional committee that investigated January 6, was soon after censured by the Republican National Committee. The Illinois congressman quickly became persona non grata in the party he used to call home.

Kevin McCarthy, the GOP's House leader, made his own contribution to the counternarrative, boasting that the FBI and Senate investigators found "no involvement" between Trump and the January 6 violence. McCarthy's conclusions were entirely made up, and there were no such findings.[39]

In September 2021, a group of House Republicans, led in part by Georgia's Marjorie Taylor Greene, held an event outside the Justice Department, heralding the January 6 insurrectionists as "political prisoners,"[40] while House GOP leaders held a separate event trying to shift blame for the assault onto Speaker Nancy Pelosi.

The *Washington Post*'s Dana Milbank noted that the developments "made explicit what has become more obvious by the day: Republicans stand with those who attempted a violent coup on Jan. 6."[41] Pointing to the sizable number of GOP officials pushing the line, the columnist added, "And it's not just the wingnuts."

Complicating matters, Republican officials didn't just want to obscure the facts about what transpired when Trump supporters stormed the Capitol, GOP lawmakers took steps to ensure they presented arguments from a position of ignorance.

In the months that followed the attack, there appeared to be broad support for a congressionally approved independent commission, modeled loosely on the National Commission on Terrorist Attacks Upon the United States—better known as the 9/11 Commission—to examine the riot and propose steps to prevent future violence. National polling showed strong public support for the idea,[42] and opponents struggled to come up with persuasive arguments against it.

Republican leaders raised procedural and logistical concerns in the hopes of ensuring that there would be equal GOP representation among the commission's members and staff, as well as partisan influence over subpoenas. Democratic leaders agreed to each of the demands.

Republicans nevertheless refused to take yes for an answer, and party leaders told their members to oppose the plan to create a commission, despite the fact that the GOP had just helped negotiate the terms of a bipartisan deal. In the House, 83 percent of Republicans balked at the idea of an independent, bipartisan commission,[43] and in the Senate, the plan was ultimately derailed by a Republican filibuster. As the measure reached the floor, Senate Minority

Leader Mitch McConnell told wavering GOP members that he would consider it "a personal favor" if they helped kill the proposal.[44]

The party had already decided to wage war on the recent past. There was no point in letting factual information get in the way.

The House's Democratic majority soon after created the United States House Select Committee on the January 6 Attack on its own and invited Republican leaders to choose GOP members for the panel. McCarthy picked five members, two of whom Speaker Pelosi rejected for being anti-election radicals,[45] though Democrats were willing to accept the other three Republicans chosen for the panel. Outraged, GOP leaders quickly announced a boycott of the committee.

The decision left the party with no influence over the probe, or even basic information about its progress and direction. A year later, a senior House GOP aide conceded that the party had "absolutely" made "a strategic mistake" by leaving itself in the dark.[46]

Democrats ultimately found two Republican members willing to serve on the committee—Illinois's Kinzinger and Representative Liz Cheney of Wyoming—and the majority party made the congresswoman, a former member of the House GOP leadership, the investigatory panel's cochair. Collectively, in December 2022, the committee released a devastating 814-page report on its findings.[47]

"The central cause of January 6th was one man, former President Donald Trump, whom many others followed," the bipartisan group of lawmakers explained. "None of the events of January 6th would have happened without him."

———

In the abstract, it's easy to understand why Republicans concluded that they didn't have much of a choice when it came to January 6. To leave the truth intact would've meant accepting the fact that the party and its president not only tried to overturn the results of a free and fair national election, they also rejected the foundational principles of American democracy.

When their efforts faltered, a Republican president urged radicals to join his crusade, roused them with ugly lies, and incited an insurrectionist riot in the hopes of preventing election results from being certified. For all intents and purposes, Trump violently swung a sledgehammer at his own country's system of government because most of his fellow citizens preferred his rival.

It was, by many measures, the most serious scandal in U.S. history: a political leader, rebuked by his constituents, acted on his authoritarian desires and took steps to hold power by force. When his party had an opportunity to act responsibly, honor their oaths of office, hold President Madness accountable, and put their corrupted leader behind them, the vast majority of its members refused.

The story of January 6 raised compelling questions about whether the contemporary GOP was still a political party at all, or whether it'd made the transition to personality cult indifferent to the rule of law. Rewriting that story was seemingly impossible but politically necessary.

And so, an evolving counternarrative unfolded, at times clumsily. Americans were supposed to blame Antifa. Or maybe Vice President Mike Pence.[48] Or perhaps Nancy Pelosi.[49] Or maybe rascally "informants" within the FBI,[50] whom several congressional Republican said existed for reasons they struggled to explain. The rioters deserved to be held accountable, the public was told, except when they were being persecuted for participating in a harmless protest.

As relevant as the details were, the bottom line remained the same: Republicans wanted Americans to believe the truth about January 6 was at odds with everything they saw, heard, and learned.

Several months after the riot, conservative columnist George Will told a national television audience, "I would like to see January 6 burned into the American mind as firmly as 9/11, because it was that scale of a shock to the system."[51] Republicans were determined to prevent that from happening.

The further the political world got from the events, the more the GOP hoped to take advantage of fading memories. In 2023, a *New York Times* investigation shined a light on "a far-right ecosystem of true believers" who embraced a "through-the-looking-glass narrative" on Jan. 6.[52] Their conspiratorial vision was bizarre, but it received ample support from elected officials, including Trump.

Indeed, the former president frequently looked for ways to add inflammatory details to the party's revised version of reality. He eventually took a keen interest in a rioter named Ashli Babbitt.

During the attack, a group of insurrectionists reached a doorway that led to a House chamber hallway. That passageway was an escape route for lawmakers who, on January 6, could see the attackers through glass windows.[53]

Rioters smashed those windows, and one of them, Babbitt,

tried to break through to enter the hallway where members of Congress were being evacuated. Officers saw her and asked her to stand down. She refused. A police officer eventually fired a single shot, and Babbitt later died at a local hospital.

Representative Markwayne Mullin, a year before the Oklahoma Republican's election to the Senate, was a witness to the developments and conceded publicly that the officer "did what he had to do" and "didn't have a choice."[54] What's more, the U.S. Capitol Police cleared the lieutenant who fired the shot, and the Justice Department officials who examined the matter determined that charges against the officer were not warranted.[55]

For Trump, however, this was just another part of the story in need of an overhaul.

In the immediate aftermath of January 6, most leading Republicans, including the former president, didn't seem to care about the circumstances surrounding Babbitt's death.[56] She was of great interest to the far-right fringe, but at least initially, the party did not see her story as worthy of exploitation. Trump also didn't see the need to lash out at the police officer who protected dozens of lawmakers and their aides.

But in June 2021, the former president said that he saw Babbitt as an ally who was on his "side."[57] A month later, pointing to no evidence whatsoever, he said the rioter was "innocent."[58] A month after that, he accused the officer who shot her of "murder."[59]

By February 2023, any sense of subtlety had been abandoned entirely: Trump told the public to see the cop as a "thug" and a "coward" who deserved to be vilified.[60]

In advance of the 2024 presidential nominating contests,

the GOP's most powerful voice continued to find strange ways to up the ante, releasing a song with January 6 inmates,[61] headlining multiple fundraisers for January 6 defendants,[62] and even coming up with an inflammatory new label for incarcerated rioters.

"I call them the J6 hostages, not prisoners," the Republican said at a campaign event in Texas. "I call them the hostages, what's happened. And it's a shame."[63]

Oddly enough, "shame" seemed like an appropriate choice of word, though not for the reasons the former president had in mind.

In December 2023, Trump even boasted that there was a "peaceful" process when he left office,[64] a claim his former secretary of state, Mike Pompeo, soon echoed, declaring during congressional testimony, "We did have a peaceful transition of power from the Trump administration to the Biden administration and I was present for that."[65]

They must have realized that the American mainstream's memories weren't nearly that short, though they apparently expected to get away with such brazenness anyway.

GOP lawmakers struggled to keep up, though they certainly tried. In June 2023, for example, Florida's Matt Gaetz organized a fake congressional hearing in which he pretended to be a chairman and called January 6 defendants as "witnesses" who were presented as martyrs to a far-right cause.[66] Around the same time, Republican congressman Barry Loudermilk of Georgia announced plans to investigate the January 6 committee's investigation.[67]

In September 2023, Representative Victoria Spartz declared her belief that the storming of the Capitol was really just a family affair. "A lot of good Americans from my district came here because they are sick and tired of this government not serving them," the Indiana Republican said. "They came with strollers and the kids."[68]

A few months earlier, Georgia's Marjorie Taylor Greene unveiled an impeachment resolution targeting prosecutor Matthew Graves, the U.S. attorney for the District of Columbia, not because he'd been caught up in a damaging controversy, but because he'd filed charges against January 6 rioters.[69]

The effort never gained traction—impeaching a prosecutor for charging suspected criminals is a tough sell—but four House Republicans signed on as cosponsors to the congresswoman's measure.

But when it came to the larger effort to rewrite the story of January 6, it was Kevin McCarthy, before his ouster as House speaker, who broke dramatic new ground in 2023. The California Republican, who'd spent months downplaying the significance of the riot, gave Fox News' Tucker Carlson exclusive access to thousands of hours of Capitol surveillance footage.[70] The pushback was immediate: mainstream observers deemed it indefensible for McCarthy to create such an opportunity for a far-right television personality who'd repeatedly told his viewers that "deep state" FBI operatives orchestrated the insurrectionist violence as a "false flag" operation.[71]

There were also all kinds of security concerns associated with the move. Senate Majority Leader Chuck Schumer wrote to his colleagues that McCarthy was "needlessly exposing the Capitol complex to one of the worst security risks since 9/11," in part by offering a media provocateur "a treasure trove of closely held information about how the Capitol complex is protected," and in part by revealing the location of security cameras across the Capitol grounds.

The speaker shrugged. After all, the story of January 6 wasn't going to rewrite itself, so as far as the GOP leader was concerned, steps like these were unavoidable.

As expected, Carlson and his team cherry-picked footage that was designed to bolster the counternarrative that the Fox host had pushed for two years.[72] The result was a broadcast in which viewers were assured that while there were some bad apples among the rioters, most were peaceful "sightseers."[73]

In fact, to hear Carlson tell it, there was no "riot" at all.[74]

As if on cue, Trump pointed to the Fox News broadcasts as proof that the official January 6 committee findings were a "sham." Referring to himself in third person for reasons unknown, the former president added that, thanks to Carlson and McCarthy, the public could take comfort in the fact that "'Trump' and most others are totally innocent."[75]

"A whole new, and completely opposite, picture has now been indelibly painted," Trump added by way of his social media platform. "The Unselect Committee LIED, and should be prosecuted for their actions."[76] The following morning, the Republican went a little further still with an all-caps follow-up missive: "LET THE JANUARY 6 PRISONERS GO. THEY WERE CONVICTED, OR ARE AWAITING TRIAL, BASED ON A GIANT LIE, A RADICAL LEFT CON JOB."[77]

As a substantive matter, the assertions were ludicrous, but for the larger misinformation campaign, they were critical: McCarthy provided the matches; Carlson lit the flame; and Trump fanned the embers in the hopes of convincing as many people as possible that the reality of January 6 was no longer reliable.

U.S. Capitol Police chief Thomas Manger saw the Fox program and was decidedly unimpressed, writing a memorandum that accused Carlson on spreading "offensive and misleading conclusions" about the attack, adding, "The program conveniently cherry-picked from the calmer moments of our 41,000 hours of video. The commentary fails to provide context about the chaos and violence that happened before or during these less tense moments."[78]

The chief went on to note that the controversial television personality and his team "never reached out to the Department to provide accurate context." Some of the host's assertions, Manger concluded, were "outrageous and false."

Republicans—by reputation, traditional allies to law enforcement—ignored the concerns. It wasn't long before House Republican Conference chair Elise Stefanik championed legislation to "expunge" Trump's January 6 impeachment. The goal, the New York congresswoman said, would be to make it "as if such articles of impeachment had never passed the full House of Representatives" in the first place.[79]

The former president's impeachment was a stain on his already tarnished legacy, and Stefanik's measure—which quickly picked up eleven GOP cosponsors and received public encouragement from the party's House leadership—intended to wash it away. A bipartisan majority had held Trump accountable, and many in his party were determined to undo what had been done, adding a preposterous chapter to the rewritten recent history.

Republicans assumed their propaganda campaign would prove effective, at least with their base, and with good reason.

In February 2021, national polling found that most Trump voters believed the "blame Antifa" talking point.[80] Two months later, a Reuters poll similarly found that half of the nation's GOP voters believed that the Capitol assault was either a nonviolent protest or was a riot launched by left-wing activists "trying to make Trump look bad."[81]

The more time passed, the more disheartening the data appeared. In October 2021, a Quinnipiac University survey asked respondents, "Do you consider what happened at the U.S. Capitol on January 6th an attack on the government, or not?" The poll found that two-thirds of Republicans believed the latter.[82] Two months later, a survey from YouGov and CBS News similarly showed that 67 percent of Republicans did not consider the Jan. 6 riot an attempt "to overturn the election and keep Donald Trump in power."[83]

A partisan consensus soon took root. In 2022, a Monmouth University poll found that 77 percent of Republicans said January 6 wasn't an "insurrection," while 51 percent didn't even consider the attack a "riot."[84] A year later, a national poll conducted by YouGov and *The Economist* found that a majority of GOP voters—and three-fifths of Trump voters—agreed that those who attacked the Capitol were engaged "in legitimate political discourse."[85] The same data showed that more than seven in ten Trump voters believed that the former president bore little or no responsibility for the violence.

A *Washington Post*–University of Maryland poll later found that more than a third of GOP voters, and nearly half of Trump's supporters, believed that FBI operatives "organized and encouraged" the attack on the Capitol, shifting responsibility from the rioters to federal law enforcement.[86]

Assessing the significance of the polling data in October 2023, *The Atlantic*'s Ron Brownstein argued that the United States "now faces the possibility of sustained threats to the tradition of free and fair elections, with Trump's own anti-democratic tendencies not only tolerated but amplified by his allies across the party."[87]

It's this point that helps drive home the prolonged significance of the Capitol riot. At issue was the most serious attack on the country's seat of government since 1814. This wasn't a "protest" that spiraled out of control, and it certainly wasn't a group of "tourists" who visited Capitol Hill with "strollers" in tow.

Rather, this was a violent and organized offensive, launched by a desperate and flailing president who wanted to stay in office despite the verdict of his own country's voters. The Republican Party deemed these unsatisfying truths to be in need of a rewrite, concluding that they could get away with cascading deceptions: lies about the election results, followed by a second round of lies about the violence committed by those who believed the GOP's first set of lies.

When sentencing the Trump supporter who accosted Officer Fanone on January 6, U.S. District Judge Amy Berman Jackson not only contextualized the circumstances, she also emphasized the importance of sending a message to future radicals.

"People need to understand that they can't do this, or anything like this, again," the jurist explained during a sentencing hearing in October 2022.[88] "They can't try to force their will on the American people once the American people have already spoken at the ballot box. That's the opposite of democracy—it's tyranny. And the threat to democracy, the dark shadow of tyranny, unfortunately, has not gone away.

"There are people who are still disseminating the lie that the election was stolen. They're doing it today," she continued. "And the people who are stoking that anger for their own selfish purposes, they need to think about the havoc they've wreaked, the lives they've ruined, the harm to their supporters' families, even, and the threat to this country's foundation."

But therein lay the core problem: much of the Republican Party, including most of its leaders, concluded that the havoc they wreaked was ultimately irrelevant. They set out to convince their supporters to replace fact with fiction, and to accept their abuses as legitimate, and there was ample evidence—from polling data to primary election results—to suggest that their misinformation had won over their rhetorical targets.

As 2024 got underway, U.S. district judge Royce Lamberth, who was appointed to the federal bench by Ronald Reagan in 1987, reflected on the broader landscape while sentencing a man who participated in the January 6 assault. "The court is accustomed to defendants who refuse to accept that they did anything wrong," the jurist said.[89] "But in my thirty-seven years on the bench, I cannot recall a time when such meritless justifications of criminal activity have gone mainstream."

Lamberth didn't mention any Republican officials by name, but he made reference to a variety of GOP claims before concluding, "I have been dismayed to see distortions and outright falsehoods seep into the public consciousness. The court fears that such destructive, misguided rhetoric could presage further danger to our country."

The resulting dynamic couldn't be more unsettling: the GOP, in pursuit of power, abandoned democracy and accountability in ways that invited future violence. In the rewritten story, the January 6 attack was the first offensive of its kind, but it was unlikely to be the last.

CHAPTER 4

"A PERFECT PHONE CALL"

*Rewriting the Story of Trump's Ukraine
Scandal and First Impeachment*

On February 24, 2022, Vladimir Putin's Russian government followed through on a lengthy series of threats and launched an invasion of its neighbors in Ukraine. The result was one of the most dramatic international challenges of the post–Cold War era, creating hundreds of thousands of casualties, a refugee crisis, and an uprooted global marketplace for everything from oil to food.

But in the United States, there was a political dimension to the crisis that unfolded nearly three years earlier, which had a direct impact on the war itself.

The public first learned of the Trump administration's Ukraine scandal on September 5, 2019, when the editorial board of the *Washington Post* published a stunning piece alleging that the president had delayed U.S. military support for Ukraine as part of an attempt to force Ukrainian president Volodymyr Zelensky to "intervene in the 2020 U.S.

presidential election by launching an investigation of the leading Democratic candidate, Joe Biden."[1]

The editorial added, "Mr. Trump is not just soliciting Ukraine's help with his presidential campaign; he is using U.S. military aid the country desperately needs in an attempt to extort it."

What the *Post*'s editors described was, for all intents and purposes, an organized crime shakedown, launched by the sitting president of the United States. "It's a nice aid package we have here, which you need as Russia breathes down your neck," the Republican effectively told his foreign counterpart. "It'd be a shame if something happened to it."

The *Post*'s piece proved to be one of the most important editorials in American history, but the news didn't come out of nowhere. A week earlier, *Politico* published a report shining a light on the fact that the Trump administration was "slow-walking $250 million in military assistance to Ukraine,"[2] to the great frustration of officials who were eager to help the U.S. ally deter Russian aggression. But at the time, many observers assumed the funds hadn't yet reached Kyiv for bureaucratic reasons.

The *Post*'s editorial recontextualized the details: this wasn't a dynamic in which an incompetent administration struggled to honor an international commitment; it was a situation in which the White House deliberately chose not to honor a commitment because of a presidential election plot.

A few months earlier, Trump was interviewed by ABC News' George Stephanopoulos and raised some eyebrows by suggesting he was open to receiving campaign assistance from foreign governments. The president envisioned a scenario in which a politician is offered dirt on an opponent from foreign sources and mocked the very idea of alerting the FBI to the outreach. "Give me a break," he said. "Life doesn't work that way."[3]

The president added, "There's nothing wrong with listening." Asked why he'd want foreign interference in American elections, Trump went on to say, "They have information, I think I'd take it."

At the time, the on-air comments were seen as controversial in part because of his indifference to his own country's rule of law, and in part because Trump had received and benefited from Russian assistance three years earlier. He also seemed to signal to his prospective international benefactors that he would welcome their interference in his reelection efforts.

But the revelations about Ukraine put the comments in a new light: the Republican wasn't just open to the possibility of campaign support from foreign governments, he was also willing to use his office to leverage foreign governments into giving his political operation a boost.

In the wake of the *Post*'s editorial, as Congress learned of an administration whistleblower who'd filed a complaint in the matter, key details came into focus, including a July 2019 call between the U.S. and Ukrainian presidents. The phone meeting came a week after Trump directed the State and Defense departments to withhold nearly $400 million in aid to Ukraine.[4] The Republican initially shrugged off the controversy, telling reporters his phone meeting with Zelensky was "nice" and "beautiful."[5] He soon after added that the call was "absolutely perfect," and the whistleblower was responsible for a "false alarm."[6]

Reality soon proved otherwise. After months in which Democratic leaders in Congress rebuffed impeachment calls, House Speaker Nancy Pelosi grudgingly announced a formal impeachment inquiry on September 24, 2019. As the House speaker saw it, the White House hadn't left her with much of a choice: the evidence showed the president withheld congressionally approved military assistance to a vulnerable ally as part of an illicit extortion scheme.

Hours later, Trump declared via social media that he'd authorized the release of an "unredacted transcript" of the July 25 call with Zelensky, which he said would prove that it was nothing more than "a very friendly and totally appropriate call," in which he asserted "no pressure" on his foreign counterpart. The following morning, the Republican added, "Will the Democrats apologize after seeing what was said on the call with the Ukrainian President?"[7]

The White House then released an official call summary, detailing the phone meeting. It was vastly worse than even Trump's detractors expected. The five-page document showed the Ukrainian leader hoping to secure U.S. support in the face of Russian aggression, only to hear Trump say he was open to the possibility, though the American told him, "I would like you to do us a favor, though."[8]

The "favor" was a multifaceted request in which Trump wanted Zelensky to "look into" Joe Biden, coordinate with Rudy Giuliani as the former mayor sought dirt on the president's likely 2020 opponent, talk to Attorney General William Barr about the findings, and explore conspiracy theories related to Hillary Clinton.

There was nothing subtle about any of this. The Republican had presented his counterpart in Kyiv with a quid pro quo:

Trump, who'd blocked congressionally approved aid from
reaching Ukraine, wanted Zelensky to cooperate with his election plot. The White House had voluntarily shared what was
effectively a smoking gun—Trump had obviously prioritized
his own electoral interests above the nation's foreign policy—
and the idea that Democratic lawmakers would "apologize
after seeing what was said on the call" was exposed as foolish.

Making matters worse, a day later, Representative Adam
Schiff, the top Democratic member of the House Intelligence
Committee, released a declassified version of the original
whistleblower complaint in which the unnamed official expressed concern that the president was "using the power of
his office to solicit interference from a foreign country."[9]

The same complaint alleged a cover-up—White House
officials were concerned enough about Trump's comments
to Zelensky that they took steps to "lock down" a transcript
of the conversation—leaving little doubt that even many of
those around the president realized that he'd gone too far.

As the scandal intensified, congressional Republicans
generally found themselves at a loss for words. Hoping to
buy some time, Senator Pat Toomey appeared on NBC's *Meet
the Press* and said, "Look, it is not appropriate for any candidate for federal office—certainly, including a sitting president—to ask for assistance from a foreign country. That's
not appropriate. But I don't know that that's what happened
here."[10]

It quickly became painfully obvious that the Pennsylvanian was actually understating matters: Trump not only
sought foreign assistance, he also pursued his goal by lever-
aging desperately needed military assistance.

A month into the ordeal, with an impeachment inquiry underway, the American president sat down with the Ukrainian president at the United Nations. A reporter asked Trump, "Would you like President Zelensky to do more on Joe Biden and the investigation?" The Republican replied, "No, I want him to do whatever he can."[11] Trump repeated the appeal days later, telling reporters on the White House South Lawn, "I would say that President Zelensky, if it were me, I would recommend that they start an investigation into the Bidens."[12]

A variety of political observers did a double take. Facing impeachment over pressuring a foreign leader to cooperate with his electoral goals, Trump did it again—twice—and this time, he did it on camera for all the world to see.

Around this time, some of the president's allies specifically took aim at whether the underlying extortion plot necessarily included a quid pro quo. The official call summary showed Trump talking about military aid and the "favor" he wanted Zelensky to perform, but, some GOP voices suggested,[13] the American president didn't literally and explicitly say that he'd provide security support in exchange for anti-Biden dirt. If there was no actual quid pro quo, the argument went, then perhaps the impeachment effort lacked merit.

Republican senator Chuck Grassley of Iowa, for example, said, "There was no quid pro quo; you'd have to have that if there was going to be anything wrong." House Freedom Caucus chairman Mark Meadows, months before formally joining Trump's team in the West Wing, emphasized the same point via social media, publishing a variety of tweets about the absence of a quid pro quo.[14]

White House Chief of Staff Mick Mulvaney nevertheless proceeded to shred this line of argument in October 2019, telling the press that Trump really did hold up Ukraine aid for political reasons. "I have news for everybody: Get over it," he said. "There's going to be political influence in foreign policy."[15]

When a reporter explained to Mulvaney that he'd "just described a quid pro quo," the chief of staff replied, "We do that all the time with foreign policy."

A congressional Republican described the comments as "totally inexplicable," adding, "He literally said the thing the president and everyone else said did not happen."[16] Marveling at the confession, Democrat Adam Schiff added, "Mr. Mulvaney's acknowledgment means that things have gone from very, very bad to much, much worse."

The chief of staff tried to reverse course a few hours later,[17] issuing a statement that said the opposite of what he'd articulated in the White House press briefing room earlier that afternoon, but by that point it was too late.

It wasn't just the chief of staff. Bill Taylor, Trump's top diplomat to Ukraine, told Congress that Trump was directly involved in an explicit scheme to leverage both military aid and a White House meeting as part of a plan to coerce Ukraine into participating in Trump's political scheme.[18]

A week later, Lieutenant Colonel Alexander Vindman, the top Ukraine expert on the White House National Security Council, told lawmakers that he personally listened in on the Trump-Zelensky call as part of his official duties. "I was concerned by the call," he testified. "I did not think it was proper to demand that a foreign government investigate a U.S. citizen, and I was worried about the implications for the U.S. government's support of Ukraine."[19]

Gordon Sondland, the Trump administration's ambassador to the European Union, proceeded to tell House impeachment investigators that he told a Ukrainian official U.S. military aid had been locked—and to unlock it, the administration expected Kyiv to move forward with the anti-Biden investigation, which Trump could then use for domestic political purposes.[20]

David Holmes, a career foreign service officer, told congressional investigators he overheard a phone conversation in which Trump personally pressed Sondland about whether the Ukrainian government would help him go after Biden.[21]

As the impeachment inquiry in the House proceeded, attention turned to testimony from witnesses requested specifically by Republican members of the Judiciary Committee. The expectation was that they'd provide information that cast the White House in a more favorable light. The opposite happened: Tim Morrison, the former top National Security Council official for Russia and European affairs, said he heard Sondland tell a top Zelensky aide that Ukraine would have to announce an anti-Biden investigation "as a condition" before the Trump administration would lift its hold on military support.[22]

The same week, the *Washington Post* uncovered hundreds of documents from the White House Counsel's Office, showing that after the impeachment inquiry began, Trump aides scrambled to "generate an after-the-fact justification for the decision" the president had already made to block assistance for Ukraine.[23] A related *New York Times* report added that after the White House put a hold on aid to Ukraine, Mulvaney asked budget officials "whether there was a legal justification" that might defend the steps the president had already taken.[24]

As the congressional hearings came to an end, the scandal was sorely lacking in ambiguities. It was as if the political world had played a game of *Clue*, and investigators had solved the case and identified the culprit: it was the desperate president, in the West Wing, with his phone. Each of the relevant players knew who was responsible for the misdeeds. The questions about how, when, and why the misdeeds were committed had clear answers. The riddle had a solution.

The Associated Press published a rather brutal analysis shortly before Thanksgiving 2019, highlighting the "mountain of evidence" that was uncontested and "beyond dispute."[25] The facts, the AP added, were "confirmed by a dozen witnesses, mostly staid career government officials who served both Democratic and Republican administrations. They relied on emails, text messages and contemporaneous notes to back up their recollections."

The *Washington Post*'s Eugene Robinson wrote in an opinion column the same day, "After this week's impeachment testimony, if Republicans continue to insist that Dear Leader President Trump did absolutely nothing wrong—and they might do just that—then the GOP has surrendered any claim to being a political party. It would be a full-fledged cult of personality."[26]

It was also on that day when *Politico* reported, "Even as Democrats felt that they had made an ironclad case that Trump had abused the power of his office by pressuring a foreign government to interfere in the 2020 election, they were no closer to persuading even a single House Republican to join them in voting to impeach the president."[27]

To the extent that GOP lawmakers turned to Trump to provide them with defenses they could use on his behalf, the president was little use. On the eve of his impeachment, the Republican wrote a hysterical letter to the House speaker, accusing Pelosi of having "cheapened the importance of the very ugly word, impeachment" and said she was "declaring open war on American Democracy" by taking steps to hold him accountable for obvious wrongdoing.

It was as if people close to Trump saw him on the verge of a breakdown, encouraged him to unburden himself, and sat back as he did exactly that, in writing—tying together self-pity, conspiracy theories, idiosyncratic grammar, and a primal scream—at which point he thought it'd be a good idea to send his stream-of-consciousness tantrum to Capitol Hill.

Rick Wilson, a longtime Republican strategist, said Trump's letter was "pure crazy, weapons-grade nuts."[28] Kevin M. Kruse, a professor of history at Princeton University, added that future scholars would need to be assured that the official White House correspondence "was not, in fact, a crayon-scribbled manifesto discovered in the shack of a lunatic."[29]

Or put another way, as lawmakers prepared to vote on his impeachment, the sitting president simply couldn't think of an intelligible defense for his actions.

Those looking for an excuse to brush off the revelations also found little help from outside Capitol Hill. Ahead of the floor vote in the House, more than 750 legal scholars issued a joint statement concluding that Trump was guilty of "impeachable conduct."[30] They added, "His conduct is precisely the type of threat to our democracy that the Founders feared when they included the remedy of impeachment in the Constitution." Soon after, an even larger group of historians signed on to a related statement, condemning the president's "flagrant abuses of power" and insisting that his actions "urgently and justly require his impeachment."[31]

For congressional Republicans, it didn't matter. During the impeachment inquiry, many GOP members didn't bother to show up for depositions[32] and refused to read relevant transcripts.[33] It surprised no one when the House approved two articles of impeachment on December 18, 2019, and the measures received literally zero Republican votes.[34]

As attention shifted to the GOP-led Senate, it hardly seemed possible for the available facts to get any worse, but they did. In early 2020, the Government Accountability Office, a nonpartisan watchdog agency that conducts audits and investigations for Congress, concluded that the White House's Ukraine scheme wasn't just an abuse, it was also illegal.[35] "Faithful execution of the law does not permit the President to substitute his own policy priorities for those that Congress has enacted into law," the GAO found.

Senator Patrick Leahy, in his forty-fifth year on Capitol Hill, said in reference to the GAO's findings, "I have never seen such a damning report in my life." The Vermont Democrat added, "I read it twice."

Around the same time, John Bolton, Trump's former White House national security advisor, leaked word that he, Defense Secretary Mark Esper, and Secretary of State Mike Pompeo privately urged the president over the summer to pursue a more responsible course on U.S. policy toward Kyiv.[36] Trump, in Bolton's telling, refused.

All the while, the president's penchant for dishonesty managed to get worse. As the Republican obsessively told the public that he was part of "a perfect phone call" with the Ukrainian leader, CNN's Daniel Dale examined Trump's defenses related to the scandal and found a president who was guilty of "compulsive" mendacity.[37] "President Donald Trump is dishonest about a whole lot of things. But he is rarely as comprehensively dishonest as he has been about his dealings with Ukraine and the impeachment process," the CNN factchecker explained.

A related *Washington Post* report added that the president had made falsehoods "central" to his impeachment defense, pushing a series of demonstrable lies that "crashed headlong" into reality.[38]

Complicating matters, Republicans put themselves at a rhetorical disadvantage before the impeachment trial even began. After the controversy first erupted, many went on record saying that if Trump had tried to extort a U.S. ally with a quid pro quo scheme, that might very well be a bridge too far.[39] Those comments, however, came before an avalanche of evidence landed on top of the Oval Office.

It left the party in an uncertain position after Trump was

formally impeached. To resolve the conflict, several prominent GOP voices tried to thread a difficult needle: the president was guilty, they effectively conceded, but the misdeeds didn't warrant removal from office.

Republican senator Lamar Alexander, for example, said in a written statement that Trump's guilt had "already been proven"; the president's actions were clearly "inappropriate"; and the House impeachment managers successfully proved their case.[40] The Tennessean said he'd vote to acquit anyway.

Alexander had some company in the partisan Senate contingent. Alaska's Lisa Murkowski, Ohio's Rob Portman, and Pennsylvania's Pat Toomey drew similar conclusions and made no effort to deny what was plainly true.[41] But while each rejected the validity of Trump's woeful defenses, and conceded that the allegations had merit, they also said they weren't comfortable removing their party's president from office.

Those attitudes were echoed by GOP voters. An early January poll conducted by the Pew Research Center found that roughly a third of rank-and-file Republicans at the national level agreed that Trump crossed legal lines with his scheme, but most of those voters wanted him to remain in office anyway.[42]

Ultimately, following a trial in which some GOP senators ignored oral arguments—Kentucky's Rand Paul was seen doing crossword puzzles,[43] despite having sworn an oath to take the process seriously—and the president's lawyers focused on procedural concerns in order to avoid focusing on their client's actions, Trump was acquitted. Senator Mitt

Romney of Utah was the sole GOP senator to vote "guilty" on one of the impeachment articles.

Two days later, the president condemned what had transpired as a "hoax." It was an opening shot in the war on the recent past.

Rewriting the story of the ordeal was a seemingly impossible task. The party was reluctant to let the scandal go unchallenged—2020 was an election year, after all—but they'd spent months trying to find a flaw in the case and come up empty. There was no credible counternarrative. Trump did what he was accused of doing.

Republicans settled on a brute-force rhetorical strategy built on playing a shameless game of make-believe. The public had just seen the facts presented in unflinching detail. In the GOP's counternarrative, Democrats failed to make their case, rushed an unjust process without cause, and engaged in congressional overreach for purely partisan reasons.

At times, it led the party to adopt a head-spinning up-is-down, day-is-night posture. Republican representative Debbie Lesko of Arizona, for example, was asked whether she believed it was all right for an American president to ask a foreign power to investigate a political rival. "He didn't," the congresswoman replied, reality be damned.[44] "He didn't do that. . . . He did not do that."

A reporter also asked Senator Mike Braun, "So you're saying that it's okay for a president to ask a foreign leader to investigate a political rival and withhold foreign aid to coerce him into doing so?" The Indiana Republican was incredulous about uncontested factual details. "No, I'm not saying that's okay; I'm not saying that's appropriate," he replied.[45] "I'm saying that it *didn't happen*."

Working in the party's favor, at least as far as their propaganda campaign was concerned, was a series of events that overshadowed Trump's Ukraine fiasco. In February 2020, the Senate's impeachment trial reached its conclusion. In March 2020, Covid gripped New York City, with the rest of the country soon to follow. In the months that followed, Americans confronted a series of other historic developments—George Floyd's murder in Minnesota, the 2020 election, the January 6 attack, an unprecedented second presidential impeachment process, et al.—which helped push Trump's first impeachment further from view.

But even after Biden's inauguration, the scandal remained a point of preoccupation for his party. In March 2022, after Russia's Vladimir Putin ordered an invasion of Ukraine, a Capitol Hill reporter asked House Minority Whip Steve Scalise about the 2019 scandal, and its renewed relevance in light of the war. The Louisiana Republican replied: "You look at that conversation, President Zelensky had called President Trump to thank him for the leadership that he provided. In fact, when Zelensky got elected, he said he modeled his campaign after President Trump's—and ultimately he got the relief money he was asking for. . . . President Trump stood with President Zelensky."

He really didn't. Zelensky had said a variety of complimentary things to Trump in 2019, but that was because the

Ukrainian leader was desperate for the White House's support. As for the fact that Kyiv "ultimately" received the assistance it sought, that's true, but what Scalise brushed past were the scandalous and legally dubious events that preceded the delivery.

A year later, the party wouldn't let it go. In August 2023, Republican senator Ted Cruz of Texas told Fox News that Democrats "abused the impeachment power" by holding Trump accountable for the Ukraine scandal, adding that the allegations were "bogus" and "not well grounded factually or legally." A month later, Florida governor Ron DeSantis, while competing against Trump for the GOP's presidential nomination, derided the fact that Democrats pursued an impeachment case in 2019 based on little more than "a phone call to Ukraine."[46]

The same week, GOP representative Ken Buck of Colorado wrote an op-ed condemning Trump's first impeachment as "a disgrace to the Constitution and a disservice to Americans."[47] House Speaker Mike Johnson added soon after that the 2019 impeachment was a "sham."[48]

Around the same time, House Republicans approved a formal censure resolution condemning Adam Schiff, denouncing the California Democrat for having helped launch the 2019 impeachment effort—as if this were itself somehow evidence of wrongdoing.

All the while, Republican congressional leaders spoke frequently and publicly about a radical idea that would allow the party to try to erase the matter from the *Congressional Record* altogether, even if it couldn't erase the scandal and its consequences from our memories.

Indeed, as the impeachment proceedings neared their end in the Senate, Speaker Pelosi acknowledged the fact that the president's Republican allies were likely to acquit him, but she quickly added that such a verdict would not invalidate the process or render the charges irrelevant.

"I think that we have pulled back a veil of behavior totally unacceptable to our founders, and that the public will see this with a clearer eye, an unblurred eye," the California Democrat said in February 2020, referring to the president.[49] Pelosi added, "Whatever happens, he has been impeached forever."

The assessment certainly made sense. For Trump's critics, the Ukraine scandal that led to his impeachment left a stain that would not wash off. The debacle would not soon fade from memory; it would instead help define his scandal-plagued tenure.

The Republican himself, however, didn't quite see it that way.

"Should they expunge the impeachment in the House?" the president rhetorically asked reporters at the White House on the heels of the Senate trial. Answering his own question, "They should because it was a hoax."[50]

In other words, as Trump saw it, there was no reason to allow the controversy to tarnish his legacy. As far as he was concerned, the underlying scandal had been discredited to his satisfaction, and GOP lawmakers at their earliest opportunity could simply wipe the slate clean by holding a vote to erase his punishment—in effect, unimpeaching him, as part of some kind of unprecedented do-over resolution.

It wasn't long before the president's partisan allies threw their support behind the effort. A few weeks after the Senate trial concluded, Republican representative Lee Zeldin told a far-right website that he believed that if his party held a majority after the 2020 elections, "one of the very first orders of business" would be "to expunge the sham impeachment."[51] The New York congressman echoed the sentiment via social media, tweeting, "EXPUNGE the sham impeachment! President Trump, ACQUITTED FOR LIFE, should have never been impeached in the first place."

After Democratic victories on Election Day 2020, the idea faded from view, only to return in 2022, when Republican representative Markwayne Mullin, ahead of his successful Senate campaign in Oklahoma, introduced a measure to expunge Trump's impeachment from the record.[52]

As 2023 got underway, talk of "expungement" lingered. Within days of earning the gavel in early January, House Speaker Kevin McCarthy opened the door to undoing the former president's impeachment, saying he "understood" why it was a GOP priority and vowing to take it seriously.[53] Other House Republicans soon followed.[54]

Six months later, the idea took the next step when Representative Marjorie Taylor Greene unveiled a resolution to undo Trump's first impeachment, insisting that the former president had been "wrongfully accused of misconduct."[55] House Republican Conference chair Elise Stefanik, one of the cosponsors of the bill, said the goal was to tweak the record, and make it "as if such articles of impeachment had never passed the full House of Representatives" in the first place.

The point of the GOP effort, in other words, was to simply take what transpired and toss Trump's first impeachment down the memory hole, as if the events had never occurred. Republicans were not content to simply vote against holding him accountable; much of the party felt compelled to erase the vote itself, rewriting recent history in the most audacious way possible.

From the perspective of the former president and his loyalists, there was no great mystery behind the motivation for the "expungement" push. Trump was caught extorting a U.S. ally, deliberately undermining Ukraine in the hopes of pressuring a foreign country to help him cheat in an election. Even his most ardent backers struggled to concoct a coherent defense.

But Republican efforts to rewrite the story—and perhaps even erase chapters the party found unpleasant—could not change the underlying facts about what transpired, even if the former president wished otherwise. (When a group of House GOP members took steps to strip Kevin McCarthy of his speaker's gavel in 2023, Trump could've tried to rescue the Republican leader but chose not to. The former president later told McCarthy the speaker's reluctance to move forward with an expungement effort was one of the main reasons he sat on his hands as the congressional leader floundered.[56])

For Trump loyalists on Capitol Hill, the truth was nevertheless pushed aside. Republican representative Nancy Mace insisted in June 2023, for example, that the basis for Trump's first impeachment was "based on a bed of lies,"[57] none of which she could identify. The South Carolinian wasn't in Congress in 2019, but she'd heard the ham-fisted counternarrative about the Ukraine scandal, and she liked it more than the truth.

To hear GOP leaders tell it, the devastating case against Trump—complete with details the party failed to even contest in a serious way—was simply not to be taken seriously. Party officials couldn't think of a way to put a positive spin on the real story, so they did what they do far too often: they wrote a new one that wasn't true.

When the party agreed to target President Biden with an impeachment inquiry of its own, his predecessor's Ukraine scandal returned to the fore in ways Republicans saw as beneficial to Trump—though the closer one looked at the details, the more absurd the effort appeared.

In 2015, the Obama administration, European diplomats, the International Monetary Fund, and other international organizations, leaned on the Ukrainian government to fire the country's top prosecutor, Viktor Shokin. The rationale behind the push—which enjoyed bipartisan support on Capitol Hill at the time—was because Shokin was notoriously lax on investigating corruption.[58] In his capacity as vice president, Biden played a prominent role in forcing Kyiv's hand and forcing Shokin's ouster.

Several years later, the Democrat's partisan opponents, determined to even the score after Trump's impeachments, clung to a conspiracy theory that Biden's efforts were somehow connected to his son, Hunter, who played a role with a Ukrainian company, which in turn lent retroactive credence to Trump's efforts.

The line of argument was literally unbelievable. For one

thing, the conspiracy theory related to Hunter Biden was wholly unsupported by evidence, despite GOP lawmakers spending a year desperately searching for incriminating details. For another, the case against Biden was ultimately irrelevant: Trump didn't have the authority to extort a U.S. ally for campaign assistance, even if the Republican thought he had a legitimate reason.

As for the consequences, the fallout from Trump's scandal reverberated in dramatic fashion, and not just in the United States. The former president's scheme, for example, left Ukraine weakened and vulnerable, and it was ultimately attacked by its Russian neighbor.

Kevin Madden, a Republican strategist, explained in the immediate aftermath of the Russian invasion, "There's just a lot of evidence that Trump was wrong on this issue, and that in many ways, we undermined . . . Zelensky's position in the eyes of Russia and Putin."[59]

Adding insult to injury, by rewriting the story, the GOP helped establish a radical and potentially dangerous precedent: future American presidents have received an unmistakable message that they can get away with such tactics, just so long as their party is prepared to look the other way.

Shortly before Trump's impeachment acquittal, Senator Susan Collins—who voted with her party despite the evidence, despite her reputation as one of her party's more "moderate" members—made the case that Trump had already paid a price that would leave him chastened going forward.

"I believe that the president has learned from this case," the Maine Republican said on CBS's *Face the Nation* in February 2020. "The president has been impeached. That's a pretty big lesson."[60] Collins added that Trump would have no choice but to be "much more cautious" in the future.

Others in the party embraced similar assumptions. Indiana's Mike Braun said on NBC's *Meet the Press*, "I think he'll put two and two together. In this case, he was taken to the carpet." Tennessee's Lamar Alexander added a week later, "I would think [Trump] would think twice before he did it again."

In July 2023, the former president headlined a campaign rally and called on Republicans to withhold military support for Ukraine until Congress received more information about the party's anti-Biden conspiracy theories.

"Congress should refuse to authorize a single additional shipment of our depleted weapons stockpiles . . . to Ukraine until the FBI, DOJ, and IRS hand over every scrap of evidence they have on the Biden Crime Family's corrupt business dealings," the former president told attendees,[61] pointing to a Democratic scandal that existed only in his party's imaginations. He added that Republicans who resisted his demands and supported Ukrainian aid anyway should face primary challenges.

Trump made these comments almost exactly four years to the day after the infamous phone meeting in which he tried to leverage military support for Zelensky's campaign assistance.

It left the political world with a couple of unpleasant possibilities. It was possible that Collins and her allies in the GOP simply had it backward, and the president had learned nothing from his impeachment ordeal.

But it was also possible that Collins had inadvertently un-covered a more pernicious truth: after Trump and his party had rewritten the story to their liking, he "learned from this case" that Republicans would tolerate his abuses, no matter how brazen, creating accountability-free conditions for the corrupt former president.

CHAPTER 5

"I DID FINISH THE WALL"

*Rewriting the Story of Trump's
Failed Border Wall Gambit*

In American politics, some issues come and go from the national spotlight, but a focus on immigration has been a mainstay for as long as there's been a United States. In a country that's earned a reputation as a "nation of immigrants," such debates—over how best to welcome huddled masses yearning to breathe free—are inevitable.

But just as the public conversation about immigration policy has been ongoing for the last couple of centuries, so too have efforts to demagogue those who want to make the United States their home. From the Alien and Sedition Acts in the eighteenth century to the Chinese Exclusion Act of the nineteenth century to Dwight Eisenhower's "Operation Wetback" in the twentieth century, efforts to target immigrants and their communities have routinely fallen far short of the nation's highest ideals.

In the twenty-first century, Donald Trump's border-wall crusade became the latest installment in an ugly pattern—

though given his failures on the subject, he was quite sensitive about it, as became clear during his comeback bid for national office.

When Chris Christie launched his second presidential campaign in June 2023, for example, one of his core objectives was tormenting his former ally, whom he helped get elected seven years earlier.

Indeed, while much of the Republican Party's 2024 field approached the former president with caution, fearing a backlash from the die-hard Trump loyalists who comprised much of the GOP base, Christie took a degree of glee in taunting his former ally—and expressed total indifference toward far-right voters who disapproved of his criticisms.[1]

The former governor's candidacy was, of course, partly about presenting himself as the best candidate, but in equal measure, he hoped to convince his party's electorate that Trump was the worst candidate.

To that end, Christie spent months drawing attention to one of the former president's most glaring failures. "He didn't build the wall," Christie argued in a Fox News interview in July 2023,[2] referring to Trump and his infamous border policy. "He built 47 miles of wall and guess what? We paid for every nickel of it, we don't have the first peso from Mexico." It was a line the New Jersey Republican repeated throughout the summer, as Christie tried to hang the issue around his rival's neck.

If the goal was to get under the former president's skin, the rhetoric was a great success. The more Christie drew attention to the fact that Trump failed entirely to fulfill his campaign promises about a giant border wall, the more the former governor's target grew agitated.

In August 2023, Trump turned to his social media platform to declare,[3] using his idiosyncratic approach to grammar and capitalization, "Reported that Sloppy Chris Christie said I only built 50 Miles of Wall on the Southern Border. Wrong! I built almost 500 Miles of Wall." He concluded his missive, in reference to his intraparty bête noire, "Loser!"

Trump's sensitivity was understandable. His failures on the subject were humiliating, and Christie's relentless focus on the former president's broken promises reminded voters of facts Trump wanted them to forget.

The truth was nevertheless on Christie's side: According to data from the Department of Homeland Security, the Trump administration replaced hundreds of miles of old and deteriorating border barriers with new and improved structures—some of the existing fencing dated back to George H. W. Bush's administration—but in terms of actually expanding barriers onto new territory, the Trump administration added roughly forty-seven miles over four years.[4] All that infrastructure, of course, was paid for by American taxpayers.

This wasn't just at odds with Trump's postpresidency claims, it bore little resemblance to the vision the real estate mogul presented to the electorate before taking office.

In recent decades, border security has been a leading priority for Republican officials and candidates, but prior to 2015, the idea of constructing a giant wall separating the United States and Mexico was not on the GOP's to-do list. The party sought increased border patrols, implementation of new technology, and stricter enforcement of existing immigration laws, not a massive, 1,900-mile barrier stretching from the Pacific Ocean to the Gulf of Mexico.

Trump dramatically overhauled the Republican Party's approach to the issue, though he didn't originally intend to.

Bloomberg News' Joshua Green reported in 2017 that as the future president's political career began in earnest, he struggled to remember to talk about immigration policy— ostensibly one of the core issues at the heart of his candidacy.[5] Members of Trump's operation ultimately came up with wall references as a mnemonic device of sorts.

"How do we get him to continue to talk about immigration?" Sam Nunberg, one of Trump's early political advisers, recalled asking a colleague as the campaign got underway.[6] "We're going to get him to talk about [how] he's going to build a wall." Longtime GOP operative Roger Stone helped come up with the idea; he and Nunberg brought in strategist Steve Bannon to help sell it; and Trump gladly followed their directions.

It wasn't long before the Republican turned the memory trick into a foundational goal that fueled his growing army of supporters. Describing his rhetorical tactics during the 2016 primary season, Trump conceded, "You know, if it gets a little boring, if I see people starting to sort of, maybe thinking about leaving, I can sort of tell the audience, I just say, 'We will build the wall!' and they go nuts."[7]

It's no secret that Trump saw no point in maintaining the pretense that he cared about the substance of governing,[8] but the idea of a border wall quickly became the signature domestic policy priority of his entire political persona. A vote for him was a vote for a 1,900-mile barrier that would separate the continent's two largest countries by population.

Mindful that many in his party were skeptical of billions

of dollars in new government spending, he also concocted a scheme in April 2016 in which he'd force Mexico to make a onetime payment to the United States of between $5 billion and $10 billion.[9] The Republican, according to his unbelievable pitch, would then use those resources to finance the wall project.

As a matter of policymaking, this was largely gibberish. The White House lacked the authority to demand such a payment from the nation's top trading partner; Mexican officials made clear they had no intention of writing such a check;[10] and the price tag of a wall stretching from southern California to eastern Texas would be well in excess of $10 billion. But by incorporating this silly element into the larger campaign promise, Trump also raised voters' expectations: if elected, he would not only curtail illegal immigration with a giant structure, he'd also implement the idea in a way that wouldn't cost American taxpayers a dime.

The plan suffered from a long list of fatal flaws. Trump assured voters that a wall would effectively eliminate illegal immigration, for example, despite the fact that most immigrants who are in the United States "illegally" are here as a result of overextended visas. He similarly boasted that the drug trade would be crushed by a wall, despite the inconvenient reality that drug smugglers focus on ports of entry, where building semipermanent walls isn't realistic.

Trump didn't care—and neither did his followers, who made "Build the wall!" chants a staple of the party's 2016 rallies. At the same events, when the future president would ask crowds who would pay for a wall, they invariably took the cue and screamed, "Mexico!"

Republican officials and candidates, who'd never seriously entertained the underlying idea, quickly became converts: border-wall construction went from fringe nonsense to major-party priority with incredible speed.

After Trump prevailed on Election Day 2016, there were some in his orbit who realized that a literal, physical structure spanning the entirety of the U.S.-Mexico border was an unrealistic fantasy. Retired general John Kelly, after being tapped to serve as Homeland Security secretary, told the public not to expect an actual wall.[11] Ryan Zinke, Trump's interior secretary, also conceded during congressional testimony that electronic monitors would be more appropriate than physical structures in some areas.[12]

Around the same time, former Texas governor Rick Perry, before being tapped to serve as Trump's energy secretary, was asked the possibility of constructing such a barrier. "Listen, I know you can't do that," Perry said,[13] adding that Trump could instead build "a technological wall" and "a digital wall."

The Republican president wouldn't hear of it. Shrugging off naysayers, skeptics, and people whose understanding of immigration policy exceeded superficial sloganeering, the new commander in chief assured Americans that he would draw on his real estate background to build a barrier, it would be a wall, it'd be tall and impenetrable, and it'd be financed entirely by our neighbors to the south. Offered multiple opportunities to lower expectations, he did the opposite.

A "big, beautiful wall" along the border, Trump said two weeks before his inauguration, "will go up so fast your head will spin."[14]

The fiasco that soon followed was so brutal that a war on the recent past became inevitable. Indeed, in practically every way that the Republican administration could have failed in this endeavor, it did, making a rewrite a political necessity.

Trump began laying the groundwork for his preferred narrative while the story unfolded. A month into his term, for example, the new president spoke at an event for conservative activists and boasted, "We're building the wall. In fact, it's going to start soon. Way ahead of schedule, way ahead of schedule. *Way, way, way* ahead of schedule."[15]

In reality, the administration hadn't begun taking any such steps; there was no schedule; and no one at the White House had any idea what he was talking about.[16] The remarks generated applause anyway, suggesting the preliminary work on the misinformation campaign was off to a productive start.

A year later, Trump assured the public that he'd secured $1.6 billion from Congress, and he would devote the resources to "new wall" construction, adding that the work would "literally" begin "immediately." This, too, was made up of whole cloth. Lawmakers had approved funds related to border security, but as a *Washington Post* report made clear, the money was "not for wall construction."[17]

Unwilling to let the truth get in the way of a good story, the president held an event in Ohio on infrastructure and referred attendees to photographs he'd promoted by way of social media. "We started building our wall, I'm so proud of it," Trump declared in March 2018,[18] adding, "You saw the pictures yesterday, I said, 'What a thing of beauty.' . . . That's what I do, is I build. I was always very good at building. It was always my best thing. I think better than being president, I was maybe good at building. . . . We've done prototypes all over and we have something special happening."

The boast was an overlapping series of lies, punctuated by the simple fact that the images he promoted were months-old photographs of deteriorating border barriers being replaced. "The images tweeted by the president were not of his long-promised wall," a BuzzFeed report explained.[19]

What's more, there were no wall "prototypes"—"all over" or otherwise—and there was nothing "special" about the Republican breaking his campaign promises.

As his third year in the White House got underway, the federal government was shut down at Trump's insistence: so long as Congress refused to fund his wall initiative, he would not allow federal operations to continue. It was against this backdrop that the president defended his position in an especially unfortunate way.

"Everybody knows that walls work," he said. "If you look at different places they put up a wall—no problem. If you look at San Antonio, if you look at so many different places, they go from one of the most unsafe cities in the country to one of the safest cities immediately. Immediately. It works. We have to put them up and we will put them up. We got to."

It wasn't long before geography-based observers noted that San Antonio is more than one hundred miles from the Mexican border,[20] and it does not have—nor has it ever had—a border wall that dramatically curtailed local crime.

The same week, as his government shutdown dragged on, Trump sat down with members of the House's Problem

Solvers Caucus—a bipartisan congressional faction that ostensibly tries to forge legislative compromises—and peddled a variety of transparently nonsensical claims about the border. One participant marveled at the president's "very serious misconceptions," adding, "I was listening to him today. He makes a lot of comments that are so untrue."[21]

Also in January 2019, with his government shutdown in its third week, the president traveled to Texas for an unfortunate photo op. The cameras showed Trump examining images taken by border officials showing tunnels smugglers had created to move guns and drugs from Mexico to the United States. The apparent point of the gathering was to show why the administration was so ardent in its demands for a wall, but it was a report in *Time* magazine that highlighted a relevant detail that the White House should've considered in advance: "Neither border patrol agents nor President Trump explained how a border wall would help stop the flow of drugs through tunnels."[22]

At the same Texas event, the media was presented with evidence of money seized by the Department of Homeland Security from a suspected criminal who had overstayed a visa. How would a wall have prevented such wrongdoing? It was a question the president and his team preferred to ignore.

Making matters considerably worse, Trump's barriers proved surprisingly ineffective. In September 2019, the president traveled to southern California and encouraged television cameras to get an up close picture of the border barriers his administration had installed, describing them as "virtually impenetrable."[23]

Reality told a different story. In January 2020, for example, winds pushed over newly installed wall panels in California.[24] A CNN report noted that there were wind gusts in the area "as high as 37 mph"[25]—which hardly constituted hurricane-like conditions. A year later, flooding ripped off gate hinges from part of the wall in Arizona.[26]

But perhaps most important was evidence that smugglers repeatedly sawed through the barriers with commercially available, off-the-shelf power tools that cost as little as $100.[27] A *Washington Post* report, pointing to unpublished U.S. Customs and Border Protection maintenance records obtained by way of the Freedom of Information Act, alerted the public to the fact that Mexican gangs sawed through new segments of border wall 3,272 times over three years.[28]

The reporting added that after smugglers breached the wall with inexpensive power tools, they created gaps "wide enough for people and narcotics to pass through." The article went on to note, "After smuggling crews cut through, they often disguise the breaches with tinted putty, making it difficult for agents to recognize which bollards have been compromised. The smugglers can return again and again to the site until the damage is detected, using the breach like a secret entrance."

Or put another way, "virtually impenetrable" wasn't an ideal adjective for the president to have brought to the public.

Taken together, the details painted an ugly picture. As a presidential candidate, Trump pitched a vision of a massive border wall, spanning at least one thousand miles, which would be made of "hardened concrete."[29] The wall would be strong and tall, measuring up to fifty feet high. It would be constructed at a speed that would amaze the public. It would be expensive, but American taxpayers didn't need to concern themselves with the cost, because Mexico would pick up the tab.

At some of his 2016 campaign rallies, Trump said that for every instance in which Mexican officials balked at paying for the project, he would add ten feet to the wall's height.[30]

As the Republican exited the White House after his 2020 defeat, Trump had delivered forty-seven miles of new steel slats, many of which were easily penetrated. Mexico, of course, kept its wallet closed. He certainly tried to deliver on his signature domestic policy initiative—the one issue that inspired boisterous chants from his throngs of followers—but by any fair measure, he had little to show for his efforts.

The ousted president and his allies had some rhetorical options, though they were limited. They could have blamed Congress for the debacle, highlighting the fact that lawmakers showed little interest in financing a medieval vanity project of dubious value. They might have pointed to litigation that interfered with construction.[31] They also could've made the case that Trump might have had greater success with the venture if he'd won a second term.

Perhaps most notably, Trump World also had the option of conceding that the president had made a foolish mistake and expressed some degree of contrition.

But Republicans found it vastly easier to simply rewrite the story—and pretend that the wall initiative was actually a great success.

In the run-up to the 2022 midterm elections, Trump hit the campaign trail and gaslit as many audiences as he could. "We finished the wall," he told an Arizona audience in July 2022,[32] which was only true if one discards the meaning of "we," "finished," and "wall."

This was hardly accidental. In August 2022, the former president boasted at a rally in Wisconsin, "We completed the wall."[33] A month later, Trump appeared on a conservative media outlet and bragged, "We built the wall."[34] The day after that, the former president told Fox News, "The wall was completed."[35]

In the weeks that followed, the Republican repeated the bizarre claims, desperately trying to convince the public that their memories of his recent term were simply incorrect. An inconvenient question lingered in the background—if Trump "finished," "completed," and "built" an enormous border wall, why did immigration problems persist?—which he and his allies addressed by ignoring the contradiction entirely.

After the 2022 midterm elections, the former president not only tried to rewrite the story of his failure—"I did finish the wall. I built a wall," Trump boasted in May 2023—he went on to try to edit the nature of his promises. "I built 561 Miles of Border Wall between the United States and Mexico," Trump wrote on his social media platform in October 2023,[36] overstating his progress by a factor of twelve. The same missive added, "This was more than the 400 Miles that I said I was going to build," despite the fact that he said he'd build at least one thousand miles of wall.

But just as glaring as watching the Republican claim

that he'd built a wall that obviously hadn't been built was seeing him argue with a straight face that his imaginary success really was financed by Mexican money that did not exist.

In 2017, a year after releasing a campaign statement about Mexico writing the United States a $10 billion check, Trump engaged in some rhetorical sleight of hand, publishing a message to social media in which he assured Americans that the neighboring country "will" pay for a giant border barrier "through reimbursement/other."[37]

No one had any idea what he was referring to, and White House press secretary Sarah Huckabee Sanders dodged repeated questions[38] about the president's plan. The meaning of "other" became something of a mystery.

A year later, he embraced related ambiguities, tweeting that Mexico would pay for a wall "one way or the other."[39] This wasn't an instance in which a politician was being coy about a delicate strategy he was reluctant to disclose too early; rather, this was a flailing president playing odd word games because he realized he'd made unrealistic promises he had no idea how to keep.

By 2019, after negotiators from Canada, Mexico, and the United States made some relatively minor adjustments to the original NAFTA trade agreement, the Republican took the opportunity to claim that Mexico was *already* paying for a border wall. "Mexico is paying for the Wall through the new USMCA Trade Deal," Trump wrote online,[40] referring to the United States–Mexico–Canada Agreement that was completed a year earlier.

It was bewildering nonsense. Unable to deliver on the

guarantee he peddled during his campaign, the president expected the public to believe that a largely inconsequential trade deal would offer tangential benefits to some American companies, and—presto chango—Mexican funds would magically appear in the U.S. coffers to be used for steel slats.

Gary Hufbauer, a senior fellow at the Peterson Institute for International Economics, explained: "It's much harder to connect actual provisions of the U.S.M.C.A. to cash for the wall, since they don't put money in the coffers of the Treasury. Any connection between labor, auto rule of origin and other chapters to the wall is pretty remote."[41]

As his reelection bid drew closer, and the president was feeling increasingly defensive about his wholesale inability to deliver on his most high-profile policy goal, Trump invested even more time and effort into urging people to believe his preferred narrative instead of the events of the recent past.

Speaking at the Conservative Political Action Conference in March 2020, the president gave his far-right audience the hard sell. "They like to say, 'All right, so he's building the wall, but Mexico is not paying for it.' Yes, they are, actually. You know what I mean, right? They are paying for it. They're paying for it," Trump said,[42] apparently hoping that repeating the phrases would turn fiction into fact. He added, "They're paying for it. And they're okay with it because they understand that's fair. But, no, Mexico is paying for it."

Around the same time, the Republican told a New Hampshire audience, "What's happening, you know, you do know who's paying for the wall, right? Redemption from illegal aliens that are coming in. The redemption money is paying for the wall."[43]

There was, and is, no such thing as "redemption money." He was apparently referring to remittances[44]—money transfers Mexican immigrants make to help family members in their native country—which couldn't finance American infrastructure projects, even in theory, because the payments do not benefit the U.S. government.

By September 2020, Trump started adding weird new chapters to his incoherent story. "Mexico is paying for the wall, just so you understand. [Journalists] don't say that. They never say it," Trump told a Pennsylvania audience.[45] "But we're gonna charge a small fee at the border. You know, the toll booths."

Evidently, the president envisioned a new system at the border in which vehicles had to pay new tolls, which would generate revenue he'd redirect to border barriers. Trump never implemented such a policy, but he pretended that the tollbooths that existed in his imagination justified claims that Mexico "is paying for the wall."

Two weeks before Election Day, the Republican sat down with Sinclair Media's Eric Bolling, and the guest declared once again, "Mexico's paying for the wall, by the way, just in case you had any question. Mexico is paying for the wall." When the host asked how that could be, Trump initially ignored the question.

So, Bolling tried again, asking, "Are we talking some sort of tariff with Mexico?" The president, apparently having abandoned the tollbooth idea, replied, "We're talking about fees. Roads."[46]

This was plainly incoherent. By that point, Trump had had four years to either implement his plan or explain why he couldn't. By Election Day 2020, he was unable to do either, so he did what he and his party too often do in the face of embarrassment: he tried to bully reality into submission, expecting voters wouldn't know the difference.

After Trump's defeat, the Republicans' willingness to embrace obviously false propaganda managed to get worse. In July 2023, Trump joined Fox News' Sean Hannity for a town hall–style event at which the former president told attendees, "Let me tell you what paid for the wall. What really helped? Mexico. They all said, 'Mexico?' Mexico paid much more than what I was asking for."[47]

In other words, according to this head-spinning tale, Trump not only successfully secured wall funding from our allied neighbor—a development that never actually happened—in this manufactured narrative, Mexico, feeling generous, paid even more than the former president sought.

The Fox News host, naturally, went along with the on-air comments, as if they were legitimate. This, too, reinforced the larger pattern: the GOP is well aware of the fact that it needs the support of allies in order to get voters to accept rewritten history as real. It therefore surprised no one when Hannity nodded in agreement, indifferent to the fact that Trump was justifying his failures with an obviously bogus story that was impossible to believe.

With this recent history in mind, common sense might

suggest that everyone involved in Republican politics would want nothing to do with the issue. The idea of massive border barriers wasn't a GOP priority before Trump's presidency, and after his failures, it stood to reason that the party would reorient its policy positions accordingly.

Except, that wasn't at all what happened. Convinced that the rewritten story was a political success, Florida Republican senator Rick Scott unveiled a governing blueprint ahead of the 2022 midterm election in which he not only demanded that Congress provide funding for a giant border wall, he also went on to insist that GOP lawmakers should name the structure after the defeated former president.[48]

Soon after, while President Joe Biden delivered a State of the Union address, two right-wing congresswomen—Colorado's Lauren Boebert and Georgia's Marjorie Taylor Greene—thought it'd be a good idea to try to get a "Build the wall!" chant going during the address.[49] (It fizzled when no one else joined in.)

As the GOP's 2024 presidential field took shape, even Republicans who used to know better abandoned their earlier skepticism, looked past Trump's failures, and endorsed border-wall construction as worthwhile. As a candidate in 2016, for example, Chris Christie publicly mocked the idea as absurd. Ahead of the 2024 primaries, however, the former New Jersey governor reversed course entirely: instead of deriding Trump for being too supportive of a wall, Christie mocked Trump for not doing more to deliver a wall.[50]

If elected, Christie said, he'd pick up where the former president left off and add more border barriers.

Similarly, in 2015, then–South Carolina governor Nikki Haley derided talk of a border wall as a pointless gimmick. "Don't say you're just going to build a wall, because a wall's not going to do it," she said. Eight years later, after having served as the U.S. ambassador to the United Nations during the Trump administration, Haley presented herself as an enthusiastic proponent of a wall, assuring GOP voters she would "finish what we started."

Other competitive White House hopefuls in the party— including Florida governor Ron DeSantis, South Carolina senator Tim Scott, and entrepreneur Vivek Ramaswamy— also made wall construction core elements of their national platforms. Two weeks before ending his 2024 candidacy, in apparent desperation, DeSantis went so far as to tell a debate audience, "We will build the wall, we will actually have Mexico pay for it."[51] The Floridian seemed indifferent to how absurd it sounded to hear him echo one of his rival's most notable broken promises.

Such promises seemed implausible. On every meaningful front—from building materials to financing to security implications—Team Trump's border wall adventure was a fiasco. But by rewriting the recent past, and pretending the embarrassing failure was a towering triumph, Republican Party orthodoxy had been overhauled in ways that would've been difficult to imagine a decade earlier.

In October 2023, Quinnipiac University conducted an independent national survey, asking respondents a straightforward question: "Do you support or oppose building a wall along the border with Mexico?" Among GOP voters, the results were lopsided: a whopping 91 percent of Republicans endorsed the idea.[52]

For all intents and purposes, the skirmish in the war on the recent past had gone exactly the way the party had intended. Trump's wall debacle was rewritten, and as a consequence, one of the nation's two major political parties is committed to an unnecessary infrastructure boondoggle that doesn't work.

CHAPTER 6

"NUCLEAR-GRADE BANANAS"

Rewriting the Story of the
Federal Response to Covid

In early February 2020, as Americans started to familiarize themselves with an unfolding public health threat known as Covid-19, Donald Trump conceded to journalist Bob Woodward that the public health emergency was far more serious than the president was letting on when informing the public. "You just breathe the air and that's how it's passed," Trump said in a February 7 call.[1] "And so that's a very tricky one. That's a very delicate one. It's also more deadly than even your strenuous flu. . . . This is deadly stuff."

Ten days earlier, the president's White House national security adviser, Robert O'Brien, told Trump, "This will be the biggest national security threat you face in your presidency. This is going to be the roughest thing you face."[2]

In the days and weeks that followed, as infections spread, hospitals filled, businesses closed, and public fears intensified, the Republican admitted to Woodward that he saw the merits of downplaying the seriousness of the escalating emergency, despite knowing better. "I wanted to always play it down. I still like playing it down because I don't want to create a panic," Trump said in a March 19 call.[3]

Some of the president's critics worked from the assumption that when it came to Covid, the hapless amateur in the Oval Office was simply ignorant, indifferent to the warnings he'd received from experts. But Woodward's recordings made clear that some of those assumptions were misplaced: Trump heard, understood, and believed the briefings about the dangerous contagion.

He just didn't want to convey the truth to the public.

On the contrary, three weeks after Trump privately conceded to Woodward that Covid was "more deadly than even your strenuous flu," the president told Americans, "This is a flu. This is like a flu. . . . It's a little bit different, but in some ways it's easier, and in some ways it's a little bit tougher."[4]

A month later, the Republican continued to equate Covid with influenza. "We lose thousands of people a year to the flu. We never turn the country off," he told reporters at a White House event.[5]

When Woodward's second book on Trump's presidency, *Rage*, arrived on shelves, it wasn't long before the president faced some difficult questions about his willingness to tell his constituents things about a public health crisis he knew to be false.

"Did you mislead the public?" a reporter asked in September 2020, just seven weeks before Trump's bid for a second term. "Well, I think if you said 'in order to reduce panic,' perhaps that's so," Trump replied.[6]

The "perhaps that's so" concession was an exceedingly rare instance in which Trump admitted, out loud and on camera, that he'd deliberately deceived people who counted on him to tell the truth about a life-and-death issue.

It was not, however, the only instance in which the Republican felt the need to try to rewrite the broader story.

In theory, this shouldn't have been necessary. Indeed, the pieces were in place for the United States to address the pandemic with a world-class response. American research universities and health institutes were unrivaled, as were the country's rapid-response capabilities and early detection systems. All that was needed was a competent executive branch capable of marshaling the nation's resources and implementing them effectively.

In practice, however, what the nation had instead was the Trump White House. In late April 2020, the president tried to lowball the number of expected American fatalities, declaring, "We're probably heading to 60,000 or 70,000."[7] By the time the Republican left office in January 2021, more than 400,000 Americans would be dead of Covid-19.

Before the contagion started spreading in the United States, the administration failed to properly prepare for the threat, making a series of preventable bureaucratic mistakes.[8] In the early days and weeks of the outbreak, the president and his team made matters worse by focusing on public relations concerns and badly mismanaging the federal bureaucracy.

In February 2020, White House Chief of Staff Mick Mulvaney went so far as to declare at a conservative conference that news organizations were starting to cover the burgeoning emergency, not because of the threats it posed, but because conspiring journalists "think this is going to be what brings down the president."[9]

In the months that followed, Trump and his allies made matters tragically worse. Governors were told to do heavy lifting that the administration did not want to do.[10] The White House had a curious habit of creating new task forces related to the crisis, which didn't appear to do any actual work, and which were quickly forgotten.[11] Trump appeared on a near-daily basis in the press briefing room, ostensibly to provide Americans with updates on the federal response, though the sessions invariably turned into opportunities for the Republican to air assorted grievances.[12] (He would later brag to allies about the briefings' merits by pointing to television ratings, comparing his audiences to that of *Monday Night Football*.[13])

As conditions worsened, public health experts delivered one message to Americans—providing their best guidance on everything from masks to mitigation to treatments—while the president habitually said the opposite.[14] Those qualified scientific professionals were ultimately sidelined and replaced with Scott Atlas, a radiologist who hadn't practiced medicine in nearly a decade, and who had no background in infectious disease mitigation. Atlas had one key credential: he impressed Trump by appearing on Fox News and promoting a dangerous version of "herd immunity" that suggested the government should address the pandemic by simply letting people get infected.[15]

Many hoped that as infections spread and the death toll climbed, the White House would eventually have no choice but to adopt a more responsible posture. That day never arrived. In April 2020, Trump halted U.S. financial support for the World Health Organization for reasons he struggled to explain.[16] In July 2020, the Republican encouraged the public not to trust the Centers for Disease Control and Prevention (CDC).[17] In September 2020, he publicly scolded his own CDC director for sharing accurate information with the public.[18]

Behind the scenes, the administration's chaotic response was, by some measures, worse. NBC News would later obtain evidence from the House Select Subcommittee on the Coronavirus Crisis that showed the Trump White House "repeatedly overruled public health and testing guidance by the nation's top infectious disease experts and silenced officials in order to promote then-President Donald Trump's political agenda."[19]

Kyle McGowan, a former chief of staff at the CDC, concluded it would "take years to undo" the damage done to the agency during Trump's presidency.[20]

Those same congressional investigators also uncovered evidence of the Trump White House pressuring Food and Drug Administration (FDA) officials to endorse a discredited Covid treatment that the president liked.[21]

All the while, as public health officials recognized widespread testing as a key ingredient to addressing the crisis, the Republican president repeatedly characterized Covid testing as an annoying public scourge. In early May, for example, Trump declared at a White House event, "If we did very little testing, we wouldn't have the most cases." He added that by doing Covid testing, "we make ourselves look bad."[22] Trump's motivations were transparently self-serving:

higher Covid statistics, calculated by accurate testing samples, led to the perception his administration was failing to control the pandemic.

And yet it was a message he refused to abandon, even in the face of mockery. Trump argued that "the whole concept of tests aren't necessarily great" because in many instances, people with the virus tested positive.[23] A week later, he visited a medical supply distributor in Pennsylvania and argued, "If we didn't do any testing, we would have very few cases. [Reporters] don't want to write that. It's common sense."[24]

The assessments were neither common nor sensible. By his reasoning, there'd be very few pregnancies if people stopped taking pregnancy tests. But Trump apparently couldn't help himself, arguing in June 2020, "If we stop testing right now, we'd have very few cases, if any."[25] A month later, he added, "When you test, you create cases. So we've created cases."[26]

It reached the point in July 2020 that Trump tried to combat the pandemic by asking Congress to curtail funding for states to conduct Covid testing.[27]

Two months later, the president sat down with reporter Jonathan Swan for an interview that might've been more amusing were it not for the life-and-death circumstances.[28]

TRUMP: You know there are those that say, you can test too much. You do know that.

SWAN: Who says that?

TRUMP: Oh, just read the manuals, read the books.

SWAN: Manuals? What manuals?

TRUMP: Read the books. Read the books.

SWAN: What books?

The Republican didn't answer, probably because there were no books or manuals that warned against excessive testing.

Meanwhile, the nation continued to suffer. Within two weeks of Trump's interview with Swan, Covid-19 was the third leading cause of death in the United States, with fatalities in excess of 1,000 per day.[29] A month later, the domestic death toll reached 200,000—a total that would double by the time the Republican departed the White House. Making matters worse, when compared with other wealthy nations, the pandemic was claiming the lives of Americans at an unusually high rate,[30] bolstering criticisms of the woeful governmental response.

Given all of this, it's little wonder why Republicans scrambled to wage war against recent history. When a party and its president make a routine mistake, it's embarrassing and can cost partisans some popular support. When a party and its president fail to respond effectively to a pandemic, and more than a million Americans die from a dangerous contagion the party downplayed for months, leaving an accurate story intact isn't much of an option.

And so, Trump and his GOP allies did what they too often do: bombard the public with counternarratives designed to mitigate the political damage of the party's failures.

One of the president's initial goals was to leverage the crisis as some kind of cudgel to be used against his likely Democratic challenger. In early March 2020, for example, Trump delivered an Oval Office address in which he told his fellow

Americans, "We are all in this together. We must put politics aside, stop the partisanship, and unify together as one nation and one family."[31]

Less than one day later, he went after his rival, Joe Biden, suggesting the former vice president had botched the federal response to the H1N1 virus in 2009. "If you go back and look at the swine flu and what happened with the swine flu, you'll see how many people died and how actually nothing was done for such a long period of time, as people were dying all over the place," Trump said roughly fourteen hours after denouncing the politicization of public health crises.[32]

The rhetoric was popular in conservative media—the president apparently got the idea from Fox News[33]—but it had no basis in fact. The Republican nevertheless couldn't help himself. "Sleepy Joe Biden was in charge of the H1N1 Swine Flu epidemic which killed thousands of people," he wrote on Twitter the day after his Oval Office address. "The response was one of the worst on record."[34]

Trump proceeded to spend several months pushing the same line,[35] trying to convince voters concerned about public health emergencies that the Democratic front-runner—and not the Republican incumbent—was the one with an indefensible record. "Biden got failing grades and polls on his clueless handling of the Swine Flu H1N1," the president wrote in June 2020. "It was a total disaster, they had no idea what they were doing. Among the worst ever!"[36]

To bolster his assertions that Biden was responsible for a "debacle,"[37] Trump claimed to have proof: the federal response was a disaster, Trump said in April 2020, because "17,000 people died."[38]

The problem, of course, was that this rewriting of the H1N1 story never made any sense. During Biden's vice presidency, the Democratic administration's response to H1N1 was broadly popular[39] and heralded as "a model" for others to follow.[40] As for the seventeen thousand fatalities—Trump exaggerated the actual total by roughly 27 percent[41]—the Republican invited comparisons that did him no favors, given the staggering Covid death toll suffered on his watch.[42]

Relatedly, the president also thought he could deflect attention from his own administration's failures by blaming Barack Obama and his team for not leaving their successors in a better position.

In early March 2020, for example, Trump spoke at a White House event and argued that the Obama administration "made a decision on testing that turned out to be very detrimental to what we're doing." He was describing a decision that did not exist.[43]

Soon after, Mitch McConnell, the GOP's Senate leader, complained that the Obama administration "did not leave to this administration any kind of game plan" for dealing with an emergency such as the coronavirus crisis.[44]

The revisionist history was bizarre. In reality, in the wake of federal efforts to combat Ebola in the Obama administration's second term, the Democratic White House put together a document called the "Playbook for Early Response to High Consequence Emerging Infectious Disease Threats and Biological Incidents"—known informally among officials as "the pandemic playbook"—and left it as a guide for successors to follow.[45]

The Trump administration was briefed on the playbook's

existence in 2017, but it was ignored. One former U.S. official told *Politico* that under the Trump administration, "it just sat as a document that people worked on that was thrown onto a shelf."[46]

What's more, during the post-2016-election transition period, officials prepared a presentation for the incoming Republican team, reviewing the steps the incoming administration should take in the event of a deadly viral outbreak. A former senior Trump administration official, who attended the presentation, was later asked whether Trump received information from the session. It wasn't "the kind of thing that really interested the president very much," the official said.[47]

To hear McConnell tell it, Obama deserved blame for not having done Trump's homework for him. It was a poor argument made worse by the fact that Obama and his staff actually did complete Trump's homework for him.

Complicating matters, Obama established a Directorate for Global Health Security and Biodefense at the National Security Council, which was supposed to be responsible for helping coordinate a response in the event of a pandemic. Amidst reports that Trump dissolved the office in 2018,[48] the Republican justified his public health personnel cuts by saying, "I'm a business person. I don't like having thousands of people around when you don't need them."[49]

When disingenuous storylines about his White House predecessors failed to make much of an impact, Trump tried to add new chapters to the story by seeking out other possible antagonists.

In late March 2020, for example, as medical professionals raised concerns about shortages of protective equipment and ventilators, the president suggested there was rampant corruption at American hospitals. Marveling at the increased need for masks in medical facilities in the midst of a pandemic, Trump told the White House press corps, "Something's going on. And you ought to look into it as reporters. Where are the masks going? Are they going out the back door? . . . We have that happening in numerous places."[50]

Months later, as the public soured on the incumbent's Covid response, Trump returned to the subject, telling voters that doctors and hospital administrators were overclassifying coronavirus deaths in order to "get more money."[51] Around the same time, the Republican declared at a rally, "Our doctors are very smart people. So what they do is they say, 'I'm sorry, but everybody dies with Covid,'" as a part of an elaborate financial scam.[52]

Asked for evidence to substantiate the assertions, the White House came up empty. "I think that's for other people to figure out," the president told reporters.[53]

When these bogus claims failed to make a significant impact, Trump sought out new enemies whom he deemed worthy of ire. Over the summer, for example, the president thought it'd be wise to clash with the Food and Drug Administration during a pandemic. "The deep state, or whoever, over at the FDA is making it very difficult for drug companies to get people in order to test the vaccines and therapeutics," he wrote online.[54] Trump added that these nefarious forces at the FDA, who didn't appear to exist, were "obviously" trying to interfere with his reelection bid.

The Republican campaign against Dr. Anthony Fauci, the director of the National Institute of Allergy and Infectious

Diseases (NIAID), was even more intense. In July 2020, the Trump White House started circulating memos to news organizations intended to discredit the celebrated scientist.[55] Democratic senator Chris Murphy noted soon after, "Don't let this feel normal. It's nuclear-grade bananas to have White House staff sending reporters opposition research on their own top infectious disease doctor in the middle of a worsening pandemic."[56]

The admonition was sensible. The reaction was not. In the months that followed, Team Trump became even less subtle in its offensive against the NIAID pioneer,[57] culminating in preelection rhetoric in which the president called the infectious disease expert a "disaster." In a call with his campaign staff, the president added, "People are tired of COVID. People are saying, 'Whatever, just leave us alone.' People are tired of hearing Fauci and all these idiots."[58]

The fact that Trump thought some of the world's most respected public health experts were "idiots" helped explain quite a bit about the administration's failed response to the pandemic.

When the White House and its allies weren't targeting scientists, they were targeting science itself, pushing miracle cures that failed to stand up to scrutiny. The efforts began in earnest in March 2020, when Trump became convinced that an antimalaria drug called hydroxychloroquine had the potential to be "one of the biggest game changers in the history of medicine."[59] At the White House's insistence, some public health officials were pulled away from more meaningful work to explore the merits of the president's hunch.[60]

"Look, it may work and it may not work," Trump told reporters. "I feel good about it. That's all it is. Just a feeling. You know, I'm a smart guy."[61]

Questions about the Republican's intellect aside—in April 2020, the president raised the prospect of injecting disinfectants into people, suggesting it might help "clean" lungs[62]—his "feeling" did not pay off, and extensive research ultimately found that hydroxychloroquine was not an effective Covid treatment.[63] Trump encouraged Americans[64] to take the medication anyway.[65]

All the while, the president went to outlandish lengths to tell Americans they simply shouldn't much care about the dangerous contagion, declaring at a Fourth of July event that "99%" of coronavirus cases are "totally harmless,"[66] despite every public health agency on the planet saying the opposite.

A few months later, as the U.S. death toll topped two hundred thousand, Trump insisted that the virus "affects virtually nobody."[67]

A week before Election Day 2020, the incumbent added that the pandemic was "going away." If real-world events suggested otherwise, he added, that was only because there was a "fake news media conspiracy" and a "corrupt media conspiracy,"[68] in which independent news organizations secretly "coordinated" coverage,[69] alerting the public to pandemic developments as part of a scheme to undermine the Republican's candidacy.

A week later, the *Washington Post* compiled a list of instances in which Trump downplayed the public health crisis. It included 201 entries, spanning a roughly nine-month period.[70]

But throughout the year, there was one counternarrative Trump prioritized above all others: the more the public soured on the president's handling of the crisis, the more he told anyone who would listen that he was succeeding beautifully. Indeed, the president couldn't understand why anyone would fail to be as impressed with him as he was with himself.

As infection numbers first started to climb on U.S. soil in January 2020, Trump said he trusted the information he was receiving from China and saw no need for concern. Asked whether he was worried about a possible outbreak, the president said, "We're not at all. . . . We have it totally under control. . . . It's going to be just fine."[71] A month later, the Republican further boasted, "I think that we're doing a great job."[72]

Trump's preoccupation with convincing the public of his prowess was hardly understated. In early March 2020, the president used social media to insist that his administration had "a perfectly coordinated and fine tuned plan,"[73] and anyone who said otherwise was not to be trusted. About a week later, at a White House press briefing, a reporter asked Trump how he'd rate his response to the outbreak, on a scale of 1 to 10. As his troubles mounted, he replied with a straight face, "I'd rate it a 10."[74]

The Republican stuck to that line as the year progressed. In September 2020, as the total number of Covid fatalities in the United States crossed the two-hundred-thousand threshold, Trump paused to tell reporters that he and his team had done "a really good job," "a phenomenal job," "an incredible job," and "a great job."[75]

At a campaign event in Pennsylvania a week later, the president referenced an imagined report card. "You know they said, 'How did you do?' I say we get an A+," he said.[76]

In October 2020, at a town hall event, a conservative host asked him what, in a perfect world, he could've done differently in the response to the pandemic. "If you had a mulligan or a do-over on one aspect of the way you handled it, what would it be?" Sinclair Media's Eric Bolling asked.

"Not much," Trump replied.[77] For emphasis, as part of the same answer, the president went on to again say "not much" in reference to how he might've changed his handling of the catastrophe.

At the time, there were 8.3 million Covid cases in the United States. The death toll was approaching a quarter-million Americans. Trump nevertheless asked voters to believe his administration's response to the crisis was effectively flawless. There was staggering evidence to the contrary.

After Election Day 2020, the larger effort to rewrite recent history became even more intense. Two months after Biden's inauguration, Senator Tim Scott reflected on the former president's handling of Covid, and despite everything that Americans had already seen and experienced, the South Carolina Republican told Fox News, "Thank God for the genius of the Trump administration."[78]

He did not appear to be kidding.

In August 2021, Trump appeared on Fox Business and boasted, in reference to Covid, "When I left it was virtually gone. It was over. It was the past."[79] In reality, on Trump's last day in the White House, more than four thousand Americans died from the virus. For him to claim the crisis was "virtually gone" was delusional propaganda.

But in the same on-air interview, the former president also took steps to turn the public against the idea of Covid booster shots. "That sounds to me like the moneymaking operation for Pfizer, okay?" Trump said. "Think of the money involved. . . . The whole thing is just crazy. You wouldn't think you would need a booster. You know, when these first came out, they were good for life."[80]

None of this made sense—no one in a position of authority had ever said the first round of vaccines would provide protection "for life"—but the Republican's conspiratorial thinking about public health policymaking offered a peek into a larger GOP perspective.

In fact, as the Biden era advanced, Republicans explored new ways to rewrite the story of the pandemic. Conspiracy theories were at the heart of their preferred narrative.

In November 2021, for example, as scientists identified the omicron variant, some GOP lawmakers suggested it was part of a sinister plot related to the elections that were still a year away. For example, Representative Ronny Jackson of Texas, the former White House physician, labeled omicron "the Midterm Election Variant."[81]

A few months later, when researchers came to realize that monoclonal antibody treatments were ineffective against omicron, the FDA pulled its backing for the remedy. It led Senator Rand Paul to tell a national television audience that FDA officials had made the decision only because of their personal contempt for conservatives. "These are the people who think we're a bunch of rubes in fly-over country, and they have utter disdain for us," the Kentucky Republican said, condemning the move as "abominable."[82]

Paul's hysterics were at odds with basic details he really should've understood. There was no conspiracy: The FDA announced that the monoclonal antibody treatments from Regeneron and Eli Lilly, which had received emergency-use authorizations, should no longer be used because they no longer worked.[83] Both drugmakers endorsed the policy change, agreeing that the infusion treatments were simply no longer effective against omicron, so their continued use no longer made sense.

When that conspiracy theory fell apart, the same GOP senator moved on to another, implicating Fauci in a convoluted Chinese plot. Asked on Fox News whether he wanted to see the celebrated former NIAID scientist behind bars, Paul didn't hesitate. "Without question," the Kentucky lawmaker replied.[84]

Around the same time, Senator Ron Johnson appeared on Fox Business and insisted that the pandemic had been "pre-planned by an elite group of people."[85] The Wisconsin Republican, who'd previously chaired the Senate Homeland Security Committee, went on to argue that the cabal that planned the Covid crisis wanted "to take total control over our lives."

This was the same Johnson who touted a drug called ivermectin as an effective Covid treatment. It was not. Ivermectin is often used to treat head lice, but according to the FDA, the NIH, the World Health Organization, the *Journal of the American Medical Association*, and even the company that makes the drug, it does not help people with Covid.

The GOP senator nevertheless promoted the ineffective medication with deceptive online videos—Johnson suggested that pharmaceutical companies were hiding secret truths that he struggled to explain—until YouTube ultimately found it necessary to suspend his account.[86]

As the 2024 election cycle took shape, Covid faded as a leading public priority, but the party's messaging campaign wasn't quite finished. "Biden did a lousy job with Covid," Trump declared in September 2023. "We handed him over a great situation and a lot of stupid decisions were made."[87]

This was the opposite of the truth, which helped explain why the former president did not identify any of the alleged "stupid decisions."

As for the greatness of the situation the Republican bequeathed to his Democratic successor, Biden's team quickly discovered upon taking office that the Trump administration had an effective plan to develop vaccines—an initiative known as Operation Warp Speed—but not a plan to distribute them.[88] One official conceded, in reference to a distribution strategy, "There is nothing for us to rework. We are going to have to build everything from scratch." Another added that the Biden administration would have to essentially start from "square one."

On Inauguration Day, Jeff Zients, newly installed as the White House's Covid response coordinator, told reporters, "What we're inheriting is so much worse than we could have imagined."[89]

In the final year of his term, Trump appeared convinced that he could overcome a pandemic in large part by thumping his chest—because that had always worked for him in the past. But as a *New York Times* analysis summarized in the crisis's early days, "The outbreak that has rattled the nation does not respond to Mr. Trump's favorite instruments of power: It cannot be cowed by Twitter posts, it cannot be shot down by drones, it cannot be overcome by party solidarity, it cannot be overpowered by campaign rally chants."[90]

Or put another way, the Republican was accustomed to responding to political crises—mostly of his own making—with a combination of bluster, bluffs, and lies. He could rewrite stories, concoct absurd counternarratives, persuade the gullible, and wait for a new round of headlines to reach front pages, at which point he'd start the cycle anew.

Covid was a qualitatively different kind of crisis. The virus didn't care about partisan spectacles and nonsense. Infections couldn't be treated by hashtags and cable-news appearances. Americans who became seriously ill, lost loved ones, or both, were not about to accept unbelievable counternarratives about the administration's obvious governing failure.

Trump nevertheless told voters not to believe their lying eyes. The more his administration failed to meet the moment, the more he and his party told Americans to believe they were delivering an achievement for the ages.

"We did a fantastic job on Covid," the former president boasted to Fox in January 2024, before complaining, "The one thing I've never been given credit for is the job we did on Covid."[91]

In the rewritten version of reality, Trump was the insightful and underappreciated hero; Fauci was the villain;

the deadly virus was mild; snake oil treatments were vindicated as safe and effective; and those looking for someone to blame should direct their fury at hospitals, medical professionals, the FDA, the CDC, the NIH, journalists, and Chinese officials the former president believed until it became politically inconvenient to do so.

Republicans launch propaganda campaigns with the expectation that they'll succeed, and when it came to the pandemic, those hopes were largely met. Quinnipiac University conducted a national poll in August 2020 and asked respondents, "Do you approve or disapprove of the way Donald Trump is handling the response to the coronavirus?" A majority of Americans disapproved, but among GOP voters, 86 percent gave Trump a thumbs-up.[92]

Around the same time, the Marist Institute for Public Opinion conducted a similar poll on behalf of NPR and *PBS NewsHour*, and the results were effectively identical: despite the disastrous results, 87 percent of Republican voters said they approved of Trump's handling of the pandemic.[93]

Ahead of Election Day 2020, a follow-up survey from Quinnipiac found that a majority of Republicans nationwide said they trusted Trump more than CDC scientists for accurate information about the coronavirus.[94]

The party couldn't quite convince the American mainstream, but it managed to use misinformation to persuade the GOP base, which Republican officials rely on for support, votes, and fundraising.

Of all the battles in the GOP's war on the recent past, this was arguably the most consequential. As a political matter, Republicans convinced themselves that Trump's and his allies' failures were actually triumphs, creating an accountability-free dynamic in the wake of a tragic U.S. response to the century's most dramatic public health crisis.

But the implications extended far beyond politics. The more Republicans took steps to rewrite the story of the federal response to Covid, the more the party's attitudes toward the larger issue took dangerous turns. The revised story of the pandemic left GOP officials and their supporters more hostile toward science, more skeptical of subject-matter experts, and more amenable to fringe conspiracy theories.

Perhaps most important of all was the degree to which many Republicans turned against vaccines.

In August 2021, Trump held an event in Alabama—one of the nation's most reliably red states, where the Republican ticket won by twenty-five points a year earlier—and encouraged attendees to take full advantage of Covid vaccines. The booing was audible and immediate.[95] Four months later, at an event in Texas, he acknowledged having received a booster shot, at which point he was again booed by his supporters.[96]

The former president has long enjoyed an almost religious reverence among his die-hard supporters, but the mere reference to safe, free, and effective vaccines during a pandemic sparked a harsh response.

A year later, the Republican headlined a rally in Alaska, and clearly wanted to take credit for the lifesaving Covid vaccines that were developed during his term, but he grudgingly conceded that "vaccine" was a word "that I'm not allowed to mention."[97]

Mindful of the direction of the prevailing political winds in his party, the former president dramatically changed direction. In June 2023, Trump abandoned his earlier positions—two years earlier, he practically begged people to thank him for the development of Covid vaccines[98]— and told an audience in Georgia that if elected to a second term, he intended to end federal funding for "any school that has a vaccine mandate . . . from kindergarten through college."[99]

He did not specify Covid vaccines. Those in attendance cheered with excitement.

The display reflected a radical shift in GOP politics. Before the pandemic in 2020, public-opinion polls found that there were few differences between the parties when it came to vaccinations.[100] There were pockets of fringe opposition, but they weren't rooted in one party over the other.

After Covid, all of that changed. By 2021, prominent Republican lawmakers in multiple states were denouncing all vaccine requirements in schools,[101] including immunizations against polio, measles, and hepatitis B.

A *Politico* poll released in September 2023 found that Republican voters were less likely than Democrats or independents to say that vaccines are safe for children. The same data showed that "as many Republicans now say they care more about the risks of vaccines than they do about the health benefits."[102]

It seemed implausible that a pandemic that killed more than a million Americans would push the Republican Party further away from scientific expertise and lifesaving prevention measures. Americans had just endured a brutal nightmare, touching on practically every aspect of citizens' public and private lives, and saw firsthand just how badly Republicans dealt with the crisis.

But for too much of the GOP, reality was no match for partisan misinformation.

CHAPTER 7

"THE GREATEST ECONOMY IN THE HISTORY OF THE WORLD"

Rewriting the Story of the Trump-Era Economy

During his eighteen-year tenure on Capitol Hill, Senator Pat Toomey earned a reputation as a reliably conservative lawmaker. Indeed, after the Pennsylvanian served three terms in the U.S. House, Toomey spent several years as the president of the Club for Growth—a far-right advocacy organization known for pushing regressive tax policies—before returning to Congress as a senator.

Unlike many other congressional Republicans, however, Toomey routinely did not see eye to eye with Donald Trump. In early 2020, for example, on the heels of Trump's first impeachment trial in the Senate, Toomey was one of a handful of GOP members who publicly conceded that the charges had merit.[1] A year later, the Pennsylvanian was one of seven[2] Senate Republicans to vote to convict Trump at the conclusion of his second impeachment trial.

But there was one aspect of Trump's record that Toomey was eager to defend and celebrate. In 2021, eight months after both men had left office, the senator told a national television audience that the Republican president's agenda "created the strongest economy of my lifetime."

Toomey added, "That's just an indisputable fact."[3]

It was neither indisputable nor a fact, but the rhetoric was common in GOP circles in the aftermath of Trump's 2020 defeat. Around the same time as Toomey's praise, Senator John Barrasso of Wyoming reflected on the Republican president's policies and insisted they "brought us the best economy in my lifetime."[4] Iowa senator Chuck Grassley similarly credited Trump with creating the best economy "in 50 years."[5]

None of this reflected reality, though the rhetoric helped capture a manufactured narrative the party desperately needed the public to believe.

When Trump kicked off his national candidacy in June 2015, his governmental inexperience was obvious—the native New Yorker had never sought or held any public office at any level—but thanks in large part to his reality-television game show, he was nevertheless perceived by many as some kind of economic genius and successful business titan.

That impression was itself a sham. In 2018, about a month before the year's midterm elections, the *New York Times* reported on evidence of "dubious tax schemes" and "outright fraud" that Trump exploited to receive hundreds of millions of dollars from his father.[6] The revelations were as brutal as they were uncontested. The Republican expected people to believe he was a self-made man who excelled as a result of hard work and a brilliant mind, but the newspaper's reporting, which was later rewarded with a Pulitzer Prize, exposed Trump as someone who got ahead thanks to legally dubious handouts.

A year later, the *Times* advanced the story, shining a light on Trump's finances from the mid-1980s to the mid-1990s,[7] a period in which he careened from one failed venture to another, losing money at an extraordinary pace. At one point, the reporting noted, Trump "appears to have lost more money than nearly any other individual American taxpayer," even as he cultivated a higher public profile, hiring a ghostwriter to write a bestselling book, *The Art of the Deal*, hoping to further convince the public of his economic acumen.

In 2020, the newspaper twisted the proverbial knife, shining a light on Trump's humiliating tax records,[8] including the fact that the Republican had not paid any income taxes in ten of the previous fifteen years—not as a result of clever accounting, but because of his business operation's "significant losses."

The *Times* added, "When Mr. Trump glided down a gilded Trump Tower escalator to kick off his presidential campaign in June 2015, his finances needed a jolt. His core businesses were reporting mounting losses—more than $100 million over the previous two years. The river of celebrity-driven income that had long buoyed them was running dry."

The revelations painted a picture of a charlatan who spent decades failing as a businessman—a loser who kicked off a presidential bid at a time when he hoped to create new marketing opportunities for his struggling private-sector operation.

Trump, as a candidate in the 2016 cycle, nevertheless presented himself, not only as a legendary private-sector success story, but also as someone uniquely positioned to deliver an economic utopia for the American public. He'd worked hard to rewrite the story of his record, creating a self-aggrandizing myth, and his candidacy offered an opportunity to take the con to the next level.

Years earlier, the Republican had created a venture called Trump University, which told prospective students, "He's earned more in a day than most people do in a lifetime. He's living a life many men and women only dream about. And now he's ready to share—with Americans like you—the Trump process for investing in today's once-in-a-lifetime real estate market."[9]

The *Washington Post* reported that Trump's sketchy operation fleeced "students," who often "maxed out their credit cards to pay tens of thousands of dollars for insider knowledge they believed could make them wealthy."[10] The "university," such as it was, was ultimately exposed as a fraudulent operation,[11] and during his White House tenure, the Republican was required to pay $25 million to his former "students"—a first-of-its-kind payment for a sitting American president.

Trump made similar promises to voters: if the electorate would only agree to make him the chief executive of the world's preeminent superpower, he'd share his know-how, put his genius to work on the public's behalf, and become the "greatest jobs producer that God ever created."[12]

Those promises proved to be as accurate as the sales pitch to his "Trump University" customers.

There are plenty of ways to measure the strength of a national economy, and for countless families, government data is far less important than the numbers discussed at kitchen tables. In recent generations, Americans have seen widening economic inequality, as the wealthy have gotten richer and working families have confronted greater financial insecurity.

Similarly, everyday Americans have struggled to keep up with student debts, medical debts, and fewer employer benefits. The challenges have become even more acute as labor unions have lost members, reach, and influence.

During the Trump era, GOP officials not only failed to address these bedrock economic concerns, the party largely ignored the existence of such problems, focusing instead on trickle-down priorities and the interests of those already at the top.

What was more, the government data didn't exactly paint a flattering picture, either.

One of the most frequently relied-upon national economic metrics is the gross domestic product, or GDP. Put simply, it's a closely watched barometer that measures the total value of a country's goods and services. When the economy is strong and growing, the GDP is higher, and when an economy is struggling and shrinking, the GDP turns negative.

In 2015, when Trump began his political career in earnest, annual GDP growth in the United States stood at 2.9 percent, which was relatively good by contemporary standards. In fact, in the seventh year of Barack Obama's presidency, Americans experienced the strongest economic growth in a decade.

Trump not only said he could improve on such totals, the Republican took the uncharacteristic step of presenting voters with specific figures. As a GOP candidate, he routinely promised "4% annual economic growth"[13]—and in some cases, he suggested his policies could push growth to as high as 6 percent.[14] Not long after taking office Trump even raised the prospect of 9 percent GDP growth.[15]

The boasts were difficult to take seriously, even at the time. The U.S. economy hadn't grown at a 4 percent rate since Bill Clinton's term; it hadn't reached 6 percent since the mid-1980s; and it hadn't reached 9 percent since the height of World War II. But Trump, pointing to an agenda he failed to present or articulate in any meaningful detail, raised voters' expectations.

That was unwise, and predictably, he failed to deliver on his unrealistic promises. Even before the Covid crisis wreaked havoc on the economy in 2020, Trump-era GDP figures were fine, but hardly record-breaking. In his first three years in the Oval Office, annual growth in the United States ranged between 2.5 and 3 percent—respectable numbers, to be sure, but nothing close to the kind of economic nirvana the Republican envisioned, and certainly nothing resembling generational highs. Indeed, GDP growth under Clinton and Ronald Reagan was far more robust.

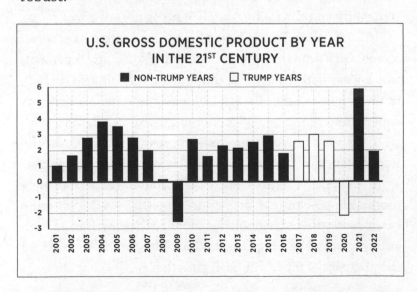

This graph, for example, highlights economic growth by year in the twenty-first century. The white columns point to the four years Trump was in office.

Data related to job growth was even less favorable for Trump. Excluding the devastating losses caused by the pandemic, the U.S. economy created roughly 6.4 million jobs during the first three years of the Republican's presidency. That's not a bad number, by any means, but during the three years that preceded Trump's term—the final three years of Obama's presidency—the economy created just over 8 million jobs.

In other words, after the 2016 election, when the White House changed from Democratic to Republican hands, American job growth slowed—quite a bit—which was an inconvenient detail the GOP was reluctant to acknowledge, and even less eager to explain.

This graph highlights U.S. job growth by year in the twenty-first century, and again uses white columns to point to the four years Trump was in office.

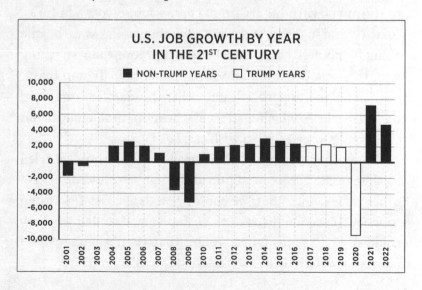

Removing 2020 from the analysis, job growth from Trump's first three years was fine. It was not, however, in line with assurances from a politician who pledged to be the "greatest jobs producer that God ever created."

While it's true that the nation's unemployment rate gradually improved before Covid took its toll on the economy, it's also true that the encouraging trend began years earlier, under Trump's Democratic predecessor.

It was a dynamic Obama who was eager to remind voters of ahead of Election Day 2020. "Unemployment was steadily going down during the Obama-Biden presidency, and then he gets elected, and it keeps on going down, and suddenly he says, 'Look what I did,'" the former president said at a campaign stop in Miami,[16] referring to his successor. "Their first three years fell short of our last three, and that was before he could blame the pandemic."

Confronted with facts like these, Trump faced a daunting challenge. The Republican had already alienated much of the public with his record of corruption, bigotry, failures, toxicity, and incompetence, but economic policy was the one thing he pointed to as a key strength. More than anything else, this was the foundation that could help Trump maintain popular support—despite the scandals, drama, and daily debacles—which made it all the more problematic that the foundation was filled with cracks.

He and his party had some options. They could've tried to change the subject and hoped the public would prioritize other issues. They could've come up with excuses for failing to meet the economic results Trump vowed to deliver. They could've tried to convince voters that their agenda would simply take more time to produce impressive outcomes.

Republicans found it vastly easier, however, to simply rewrite the story.

One of the challenging things about the GOP effort was the lengths the party and its allies went to to establish a preferred narrative while the story was unfolding. It's one thing to retell a tale once it's over; to rewrite a story as it's happening is bold—and requires a healthy dose of chutzpah.

As Trump's first year in office came to an end, job growth slowed to a seven-year low, and the United States experienced modest GDP growth far short of Trump's grandiose preelection assurances. It was against that backdrop that the president declared, "Our economy is better than it has been in many decades."[17] He repeatedly pointed to the stock market, while failing to note that Wall Street growth was actually more robust under Obama.[18]

Five months later, he nevertheless used social media to repeatedly tell[19] the public that the United States was experiencing "the greatest economy in the HISTORY of America," which in no way reflected reality. Trump, who tends to capitalize words he finds significant, added in September 2018, "We are breaking all Jobs and Economic Records,"[20] pointing to developments that plainly did not exist.

The rest of the party dutifully played along. "If [Obama's] jobs numbers were anywhere close to what we're talking about with President [Trump], the media would stop the Earth from rotating to make sure everybody heard about it!" GOP senator Lindsey Graham wrote in a November 2018 social media message.[21]

What the South Carolina senator failed to acknowledge

was the degree to which he had the story backward: At the point at which Graham published the assertion, Trump had been president for twenty-two months, and the U.S. economy had added roughly 4.1 million jobs over that period. But in the final twenty-two months of Obama's term, in an apples-to-apples comparison based solely on arithmetic, the economy generated more than 4.6 million jobs. Graham's claim turned the basics on their head.

As 2019 came to a close, and Americans started to hear reports from abroad about a contagion called the coronavirus, the *Washington Post* published a striking analysis,[22] comparing the economy under Obama and Trump at the same points in their presidencies. Republicans had reason to feel discouraged by the findings: the economy grew faster under Obama; hiring grew faster under Obama; the S&P 500 grew faster under Obama; the unemployment rate shrunk faster under Obama; and the national debt grew slower under Obama.

"If we are linking economic numbers to presidential performance, Trump's insistence that his abilities are unparalleled are rendered somewhat suspect in that he ranks second out of the last two presidents" on key economic indicators, the *Post*'s analysis concluded.

A few months later, Trump nevertheless delivered a State of the Union address in which he patted himself on the back for having "reversed the failed economic policies of the previous administration," indifferent to the truth.

As his reelection bid drew closer, the president grew even more frantic in trying to tell the electorate to trust his demonstrable lies more than the statistics made available from his own administration. Two weeks before Election Day 2020, Trump sat down with CBS News' Lesley Stahl for a *60 Minutes* interview and claimed with a straight face, "We created the greatest economy in the history of our country."[23]

The host, aware of reality, quickly interjected, "You know that's not true." Trump, unmoved, added, "It is totally true," despite the fact that it was not true at all.

After his defeat, Trump's eagerness to rewrite his economic story took a hysterical turn. In his farewell address delivered on his last full day as president, the Republican dropped his usual line about creating the best economy in American history, and instead told the public that he was responsible for "the greatest economy in the history of the world"[24]—as if human eyes had never before seen modest GDP growth and underwhelming job totals.

As he launched a presidential comeback bid, Trump clung to the transparently false claim, again saying he "built the greatest economy in the history of the world" in his kickoff speech in November 2022.[25] It was a false line he'd continue to repeat throughout the GOP primary process.

His acolytes had no qualms about reading from the same script, hoping to convince the public to believe claims with no basis in fact. The day after implausibly becoming speaker of the House, Louisiana's Mike Johnson sat down with Fox News and parroted the line he'd heard before. "If you remember, if you rewind in your mind back to right before the pandemic began, in the Trump administration, we had the greatest economy in the history of the world," the GOP congressional leader said,[26] reality be damned.

At the heart of the problem for the Republican Party was not just the fact that the former president failed to deliver on outlandish promises, or the ease with which he peddled ridiculous claims. Rather, the core concern—the motivation for the wholesale rewrite of the story of the Trump-era economy—was that the GOP *needed* its fictional narrative to be true, or at least perceived as such.

Before the 2016 elections, then-candidate Trump would occasionally impress voters by breaking with party orthodoxy on key economic questions. He signaled an openness to raising the minimum wage,[27] for example, and suggested more than once that the wealthiest Americans could afford to pay more in taxes.[28]

But once in the Oval Office, Trump quickly became a more doctrinaire partisan. Indeed, he effectively stuck to the same governing script every modern Republican president has followed: gutting regulations, scaling back safeguards, and putting ideologues with industry ties in key positions of authority.

Most important, in 2017 GOP lawmakers and the Republican White House partnered on a massive package of tax breaks that principally benefited big corporations and the wealthiest Americans.[29] The party was able to implement the precise economic agenda it wanted to impose on the country—Democratic opposition proved to be little more than a speed bump that was easily cleared—subjecting Americans to a real-world experiment of sorts: what would conditions in the United States look like if Republicans were able to do exactly what they thought would have the greatest economic impact?

It was a test the GOP created for itself, which it also struggled to pass. Not only were the economic results of Trump's presidency underwhelming, but the party's tax plan proved to be an incredibly expensive and unpopular flop.

Republicans said the tax breaks would fuel private-sector hiring, but they didn't.[30] They said their tax cuts would boost business investment, but that didn't happen, either.[31] GOP officials similarly said the party's tax policies would pay for themselves and not add to annual budget deficits, but in reality, Trump added nearly $7.8 trillion to the national debt[32] in just one term—most of which was racked up before the Covid crisis—thanks in large part to tax giveaways that Republicans swore wouldn't make the nation's fiscal outlook any worse.

What's more, once the poorly named Tax Cuts and Jobs Act was implemented, a great many corporate giants, instead of hiring more workers or making new investments, simply used their windfalls for stock buybacks.[33] It had the effect of boosting their prices on Wall Street, but little else.

The policy didn't even work politically. As the plan prepared to clear Capitol Hill in late 2017, Mitch McConnell, the Republicans' Senate leader, declared with pride, "If we can't sell this to the American people, we ought to go into another line of work."[34] Nearly a year later, ahead of the 2018 midterm cycle, GOP officials and candidates recognized the unpopularity of their tax giveaway and kept their ineffective achievement out of the party's election-season messaging.[35]

As the *Washington Post*'s Catherine Rampell summarized a year after the tax breaks were approved, "The Republican tax cut is a big, fat failure. It has achieved none of the things that Republicans promised it would. It didn't reduce deficits. It didn't target the middle class. And it didn't win goodwill with voters."[36]

It's one thing when a party takes a chance on an ambitious plan that doesn't work out as intended; it's something else when a party subjects its entire economic agenda to a real-world test, only to see it fall far short. The former is embarrassing; the latter is a disaster.

Or put another way, partisans can do their best to put a positive spin on unfortunate missteps, but when a party's core economic vision is discredited, it risks such catastrophic political consequences that it becomes necessary to embrace misinformation, replacing the story of what actually happened with an entirely new counternarrative.

Given the perennial importance of the economy to voters, Republicans found the facts surrounding Trump's record intolerable. So, they went to war with the recent past and rewrote a new story they liked better—one in which Trump and his band of GOP heroes proved conservatism right by delivering economic results unrivaled in the history of the planet.

The party's persistent rhetoric was wrong, but effective. Heading into Election Day 2020, Fox News released the findings of a national poll that found Joe Biden leading Trump on practically every issue and area of public policy—from health care to immigration, responding to Covid to making new Supreme Court nominations—but the same data pointed to a clear advantage for Trump on the economy.[37]

The same week, a national survey conducted by the *New York Times* and Siena College pointed in a nearly identical direction.[38] Asked who they trusted more to deal with race relations, national unity, and law enforcement, most voters sided with the Democratic nominee. Asked who they preferred on the economy, those same voters preferred the Republican incumbent, despite his record.

Biden prevailed in the election, winning the 2020 race by more than 7 million ballots in the popular vote, and finishing with 306 electoral votes, but it was Trump's unearned credibility on economic matters that kept the race competitive.

The effects lingered. Ahead of the 2022 midterm elections, the job market was booming—the economy created 12 million jobs over the course of Biden's first two years, an extraordinary total that was nearly double the totals from Trump's first three years—and economic growth had bounced back from the 2020 recession. GDP growth in Biden's first year in the White House reached 5.8 percent, more in line with Trump's promises than anything the Republican was able to deliver.

But stubborn postpandemic inflation left much of the public in a sour mood. A national poll conducted by NBC News in September 2022 found Republicans with a nineteen-point advantage over Democrats on dealing with the economy[39]—an all-time high for the GOP in NBC News polling.

As the 2024 election cycle took shape, the party sought every opportunity to exploit this edge as if it were legitimate. In June 2023, for example, after launching a Republican presidential campaign, South Carolina senator Tim Scott published a social media message that read, "Three years ago, our economy was thriving. Today, we're all worse off under the Biden administration."[40]

Even by contemporary GOP standards, this was a clumsy effort to obscure what had actually transpired. In June 2020, the unemployment rate was 11 percent; the economy was shrinking; and the S&P 500 index was down to roughly 3,000. Three years later, the unemployment rate was 3.7 percent; the economy was growing; and the S&P 500 index was up 43 percent as compared to three years earlier.

Yes, inflation was higher, but even as Tim Scott—who ran an ill-fated challenge for his party's presidential nomination— pushed the line, the nation's inflation rate had steadily improved to the point that it was the lowest among the world's wealthiest countries.[41]

It reached the point at which Republicans, not content to rewrite their own story, started tweaking Biden's story, too. In September 2023, Trump headlined a campaign rally in South Dakota and told his followers not to believe the official data showing unemployment falling to its lowest point since the late 1960s. The unemployment rate, the former president said, was "phony," "fake," and "crooked."[42]

As part of the same harangue, he added, "During Biden's first 30 months in office, just 2.1 million new jobs have been created." The actual number at that point was 13.5 million— Trump was off by a factor of more than six.

Prominent voices in conservative media, cognizant of their role in the broader partisan operation, nevertheless echoed the nonsense. Fox Business's Larry Kudlow—who served as the director of the National Economic Council in Trump's White House—interviewed his former boss in

August 2023 and told Trump that the economy had created only 2.1 million jobs over the first thirty months of the Biden presidency.[43]

"Right," Trump replied, despite the fact that it wasn't right at all.

The consequences of the GOP effort to overhaul the recent history of the domestic economic debate are, and have the potential to be, quite significant. Ahead of the 2024 election cycle, Republicans focused on a variety of priorities, but near the top of the list was another round of tax breaks for corporations and wealthy Americans who do not need more assistance from federal policymakers.

As part of their ineffective tax package from 2017, Republicans cut the corporate tax rate from 35 to 21 percent. Planning for a possible return to power in 2025, the party prepared plans to push the rate even lower, eyeing a 15 percent threshold.[44]

In recent years, there's been no evidence whatsoever to suggest the American mainstream is clamoring for more tax giveaways to corporate giants—there's ample public-opinion research pointing in the opposite direction[45]—but having been largely persuaded by the manipulated story of the Trump-era economy, a *USA Today* poll conducted in late 2023 nevertheless found voters trusting Trump over Biden on economic policy by a double-digit margin.[46]

Republicans had rewritten the story of a presidential administration's economic record, repeated it ad nauseam, relied on allies to help parrot the propaganda to the public, and positioned itself to reap the rewards of their successful misinformation campaign.

The stakes are difficult to overstate. The more mainstream voters look at Trump as someone who can deliver amazing economic results, the more likely it is that the electorate will look past every other consideration and return the scandal-plagued Republican to the Oval Office.

Given the electoral dominance of economic issues, the degree to which voters accept the alternate version of reality will likely have a direct impact on which party prevails in 2024, suggesting this one area of partisan propaganda may very well shape the nation's future for many years to come.

"AN ARTIFICIAL VERSION OF HISTORY"

The Dangers Posed by the Republican Party's War on the Recent Past

After television producer Mark Burnett experienced blockbuster success with the reality-competition program *Survivor*, he set out to duplicate his triumph with a similar show. He envisioned a new television series that would be set, not in a remote and isolated setting, but in an urban office building.

Instead of contestants competing in literal jungles, Burnett would have them face off in corporate jungles. In *The Apprentice*, competitors wouldn't be voted off an island; they'd be ousted from a boardroom.

Burnett wanted a big personality who would host the game show and be perceived as a private-sector titan. The producer and his team settled on Donald Trump.

At times, however, the future president was not especially good at the job. The basic structure of an episode was straightforward. Participants were instructed to compete in assorted challenges, culminating in a dramatic boardroom scene in which Trump would dismiss an underperforming contestant with a signature catchphrase: "You're fired."

In theory, Trump's role couldn't have been much easier. In practice, he was often unprepared for the episodes' big finish, having no real sense of who excelled and who faltered during the preceding competition. As a result, the host would occasionally fire the wrong person.[1]

This created a daunting challenge for the show's producers and editors. Writing for *The New Yorker* in 2018, Patrick Radden Keefe described a "retroactive narrative construction" process[2] in which those responsible for the program would comb through filmed footage, looking for moments that could plausibly be presented as evidence of a contestant's missteps.

These efforts to reverse engineer stories were necessary, Keefe added, to create "an artificial version of history" that would tell viewers what Trump expected them to believe, regardless of what had actually transpired.

In 2015, Trump launched a political career and parted ways with NBC, which aired the series. But in the months and years that followed, the core elements of narrative-construction strategy were no longer limited to the creators of a popular television game show. On the contrary, they became a foundational strategy for one of the nation's two political parties.

As Republicans take aim at the events of the recent past, they, like those responsible for *The Apprentice*, begin with a premise that what occurred in reality is merely a first draft. It's at that point when the real work begins.

What matters isn't what happened; what matters is what the party can get people to believe happened by rewriting, fabricating, and overpowering the public's understanding of recent events.

The more the party has confronted political crises it can't explain away, the more the GOP has grown dependent on this go-to tactic. In the aftermath of George Floyd's murder in 2020, for example, there were social justice protests in communities across the country, including in Lafayette Square, which is a public park just north of the White House, across Pennsylvania Avenue.

In June, during an event at the White House Rose Garden, Trump declared himself "an ally of all peaceful protesters."[3] Shortly thereafter, attendees at the event heard sounds of unrest that were audible in the background, though it wasn't immediately clear why.

It wasn't long before the answer came into sharp focus. Law enforcement had launched a rather extraordinary offensive against social justice demonstrators in the nearby park, which included, among other things, firing tear gas and flash-bang shells at those who'd peaceably assembled.

Once Lafayette Square had been cleared by force, the president walked across the park—the length of a city block—and stood in front of St. John's Episcopal Church, a congregation sometimes referred to as "the Church of the Presidents" given its history[4] and proximity to the White House.

Trump did not go inside the church. He also did not read from the Bible he carried, engage in any form of worship, deliver remarks, or even visit with St. John's pastor. Rather, the Republican held up a Bible, posed for the cameras, and then walked back to the West Wing. If there was a point to the president briefly using Scripture and the church as props, he didn't tell anyone what it was.

"Is that your Bible?" a reporter asked as the Republican posed for the cameras. "It's *a* Bible," Trump replied.[5]

In the history of presidential photo ops, it ranked as among the most offensive and most manifestly un-American. The *New York Times* published a memorable headline summarizing the developments: "Protesters Dispersed with Tear Gas So Trump Could Pose at Church."[6]

An unnamed senior White House official said that when they saw the offensive against the crowd, "I've never been more ashamed. I'm really honestly disgusted. I'm sick to my stomach."[7] Brendan Buck, a former top aide to two former House Republican speakers, added, "We long ago lost sight of normal, but this was a singularly immoral act."[8]

General Mark Milley, the Trump-appointed chairman of the Joint Chiefs of Staff, was seen in some photographs walking across Lafayette Square, while wearing combat fatigues, as part of the president's entourage. Within a few days, Pentagon sources were telling reporters the general was "horrified"[9] by the entire scene. Soon after, Milley spoke for himself, acknowledging, "I should not have been there."[10]

But perhaps no one was more disgusted than the relevant local clergy. Mariann E. Budde, the bishop of the Episcopal Diocese of Washington, said church officials had not been told in advance of the White House's plan and expressed outrage at the use of heavy-handed tactics.

"He did not pray," Budde said, referring to Trump.[11] "He did not mention George Floyd, he did not mention the agony of people who have been subjected to this kind of horrific expression of racism and white supremacy for hundreds of years. We need a president who can unify and heal. He has done the opposite of that, and we are left to pick up the pieces."

A day later, Trump appeared on Fox Radio and boasted, "The church leaders loved that I went there with a Bible."[12] He also argued on Twitter, "People liked my walk to this historic place of worship!"[13]

The rewrite was underway.

Indeed, a *Washington Post* report was explicit on this point, noting two days after the ugly scene that the White House was trying to "rewrite history," even after cameras captured the events.[14] "The president and his team have offered a string of conflicting explanations and excuses for why protesters were cleared from the area around Lafayette Square in front of the White House, what methods were used to remove them and who was ultimately responsible for the decision," the article explained.

The president had ample opportunity to respond to the backlash with some degree of contrition. It would've been easy for officials to concede that conditions needlessly spiraled out of hand. The White House instead preferred to target reality in roughly the same way protestors in Lafayette Square were treated: with unjustified aggression.

One of the first claims was that the park was cleared as part of an effort to enforce a local curfew. That defense was quickly proven false.[15] Kellyanne Conway, a prominent figure on the Republican's team, argued soon after that Trump's photo op in front of St. John's didn't deserve to be seen as a photo op. That obviously wasn't true, either.[16]

There were some suggestions that the strong-armed offensive against peaceful protestors was unrelated to the president's block-long stroll. Given the available facts, this appeared impossible to believe.[17] The White House went on to make the case that security forces might've acted in self-defense. That wasn't even close to being true.[18]

(Nearly a year later, the Department of the Interior claimed that the offensive was related to the installation of security fencing near the park,[19] suggesting that the president simply exploited the opportunity once it was available. This, oddly enough, was never pitched by Team Trump amidst the uproar.)

White House Press Secretary Kayleigh McEnany went so far as to argue that the scene was similar to Winston Churchill "inspecting the bombing damage" during World War II.[20] And while it was true that the wartime prime minister did venture out onto English streets after German blitzes, there was no record of British security forces launching an offensive against local citizens in a public park or 10 Downing Street taking advantage so Churchill could safely pose for the cameras.

Within hours of McEnany's comments, Trump boasted that the clearing of Lafayette Square was "handled very well."[21] The evidence to the contrary was overwhelming.

But as offensive as the creation of a counternarrative was, adding to the brazenness was the timing: the president's ugly stroll to St. John's Episcopal was on June 1. It received extensive coverage from domestic and international media outlets, and there were no real ambiguities about one of the defining moments of Trump's troubled term.

His "handled very well" comments came on June 3—roughly forty-eight hours after Lafayette Square was cleared. The Republican and his White House wasted no time in effectively telling Americans, *We know what you just saw, but we'll now tell you what to believe.*

If Trump expected this to help him win a second term, the

electorate rendered a different verdict on Election Day 2020. The former president launched an unprecedented campaign to rewrite the story of that election cycle (see chapter 2) then did the same thing two years later, after the 2022 midterm elections.

By any fair measure, the cycle was an unexpectedly good one for Democrats. Historical modeling suggested that Joe Biden's party needed to prepare itself for a brutal drubbing[22]: Between World War II and 2022, Democratic presidents in their first midterms saw their party lose an average of forty House seats and five Senate seats. Between Watergate and 2022, the results looked even worse for the party: Democratic presidents in their first midterms saw their party lose an average of forty-four House seats and six Senate seats.

While Republicans managed to secure a majority in Congress' lower chamber as part of Biden's first midterms, the GOP's celebration was muted: Democrats ended up losing only nine House seats while managing to expand their Senate majority, gaining gubernatorial offices, and even flipping some state legislative chambers. By nearly every relevant metric, it was the best midterm performance for the party, during a Democratic presidency, since Franklin Delano Roosevelt's first midterms in 1934.[23]

There was some debate in GOP circles as to whether to acknowledge the party's disappointment with the results or pretend that the setbacks were triumphs. The former Republican picked a predictable side.

"WE WON!" Trump wrote in an item published on his social media platform.[24] "Big Victory, don't be stupid. Stand on the rooftops and shout it out loud!"

His choice of words shed light on an unsettling perspective:

To tell the public the truth about election results would've been, in Trump's telling, "stupid." By the same reasoning, to replace an accurate version of events with a deliberately deceptive counternarrative was smart.

As 2023 came to an end, and a presidential election year got underway, there was little reason for the American mainstream to be optimistic about the future of the GOP's efforts. For example, as Trump's legal crises grew more serious—in the summer of 2023, the former president was charged with ninety-one criminal counts across multiple states and jurisdictions—his partisan allies on Capitol Hill eagerly told the public that the Republican, while in office, had displayed magnanimity in ways that deserved to be reciprocally rewarded.

Representative Michael Waltz insisted on Fox News, for example, that not long after Inauguration Day 2017, Trump could've used the levers of federal power to go after Hillary Clinton, but in the Florida congressman's preferred version of events, the generous and gracious president made a conscious choice to leave his former Democratic rival alone.

"President Trump took that approach. He said, 'You know what, we're not going to prosecute Hillary Clinton,'" Waltz said. "[Trump] said, 'You know what, let's move on. Let's move forward.'"[25]

It was a popular talking point in GOP circles. "President Ford decided it was best for America not to pursue prosecution against President Nixon. President Trump pretty much made the same decision and decided not to pursue any kind of prosecution of Hillary Clinton," Wisconsin senator Ron

Johnson argued. "Joe Biden could have made the exact same decision, but he didn't."[26]

For these Republicans, Trump brushed off the "lock her up" calls from his allies, preferring instead to rise above the rancor and focus on governance rather than retaliation after reaching the Oval Office. When he left the White House and faced multiple felony indictments, in the GOP's vision, it was proof that his Democratic presidential successor had engaged in the kind of abuses that Trump wisely rejected.

The entire line of argument was absurd, in part because of its obvious factual errors—Biden had nothing to do with the criminal indictments against his predecessor, some of which came at local levels, far from the White House's reach—and in part because of the degree to which the party was rewriting the history that many observers hadn't yet forgotten.

In fact, in Trump's first year in the White House, he publicly pleaded with the Justice Department to go after Clinton. "Everybody is asking why the Justice Department (and FBI) isn't looking into all of the dishonesty going on with Crooked Hillary," the Republican wrote to Twitter in 2017, pointing to questions only he was asking. "People are angry," the president continued. "At some point the Justice Department, and the FBI, must do what is right and proper."[27]

A year later, the president told the White House counsel's office that he wanted to order the Justice Department to prosecute Clinton.[28] It fell to Don McGahn, the White House's top lawyer, to tell the president that he didn't have the legal authority to do any such thing.

Ahead of Election Day 2020—nearly four years after Clinton's defeat—Trump *again* called for the Democrat's incarceration[29] and lobbied Attorney General William Barr to prosecute Clinton[30] for crimes she did not commit and he could not identify.

At no point did he say, in reference to the allegations against the former secretary of state, "You know what, let's move on. Let's move forward." Trump said and did the opposite.

None of this was kept secret. It happened out in the open. Americans saw the events unfold in public and in real time. For Republicans, there was no point in trying to override our memories with a more palatable story that made Trump appear gracious and respectful of the nation's legal guardrails.

But the party did it anyway.

"Remember, I went to the rallies in 2016, Laura," Florida governor Ron DeSantis complained to Fox News' Laura Ingraham in August 2023. "You remember them, 'Lock her up, lock her up,' about holding Hillary accountable. And then, two weeks after the election, he said, 'Never mind that I said that' and let her off the hook."[31]

The GOP, unable to justify the abuses Trump made every effort to engage in, decided to replace an accurate story with a demonstrably false alternative that it hoped to impose on the public, with the expectations that Americans wouldn't know the difference.

The same was true with regards to Trump and his willingness to rewrite the story of his own indictments, concocting chapters in which his successor was to blame for his criminal liabilities. Asked in November 2023 whether he intended to use federal law enforcement to go after his perceived political foes if given a second term, the Republican replied, "Yeah, it could certainly happen in reverse. What they've done is they've released the genie out of the box."[32]

Notwithstanding the fact that he probably meant "bottle" and not "box," Trump described a scenario in which he could exploit a new set of circumstances. If he won in 2024, he could prosecute Biden and other Democrats because Biden and other Democrats had prosecuted him. It was a new day in American jurisprudence, and Trump was prepared to exploit the opportunity and start using federal law enforcement officials as his own personal attack dogs.

There were some rather obvious flaws in the argument. For one thing, Biden had nothing to do with Trump's indictments. For another, the Republican's logic was flawed: A car thief, caught in the act by the police, would not be justified in trying to later arrest the officer who caught him. The thief could not credibly go to court and argue, "Well, the cop released the genie out of the box."

But more important, Trump was rewriting his own story—erasing the fact that he'd *already tried* to use federal law enforcement officials as his own personal attack dogs.

The *New York Times* published a brutal report in August 2022, the week after FBI officials executed a court-approved search warrant at Mar-a-Lago, exploring in great detail that Trump and his team "tried to turn the nation's law enforcement apparatus into an instrument of political power" to carry out the Republican's wishes.[33] A *Washington Post* analysis[34] published soon after highlighted a lengthy list of instances in which the former president, while in office, not only leaned on the Justice Department to follow his whims, but also Trump's efforts to push federal law enforcement to validate his "Big Lie" in the wake of his election defeat.[35]

The Republican's efforts to weaponize levers of power reached an astounding pinnacle less than a month before

Election Day 2020, when Trump publicly called on federal prosecutors to go after Biden[36]—at the time, the Democratic Party's presidential nominee who was leading the Republican incumbent in the polls—accusing him of undefined crimes. The then-president further suggested that his future successor shouldn't be "allowed" to run against him.[37]

On October 7, 2020, with early voting underway across much of the country, *Politico* published a memorable headline after Trump lobbied Bill Barr to use his prosecutorial powers to help his political operation: "'Where Are All of the Arrests?': Trump Demands Barr Lock Up His Foes."[38]

The following day, the Republican incumbent spoke to Fox Business's Maria Bartiromo and called on the Justice Department to "indict" his perceived Democratic foes, including Biden.[39] After his 2020 defeat, retired general John Kelly, Trump's longest-serving White House chief of staff, conceded on the record that his former boss "regularly" wanted to use the Justice Department to retaliate against critics.[40]

Rather than try to defend any of this, Trump treated the recent past as an inconvenience he could break down and re-create, casting himself not as instigator, but as a victim.

The degree to which the GOP base bought into the counternarrative shed light on why the party rewrote recent history in the first place. A national CNN poll conducted in August 2023 asked respondents whether Trump was facing criminal charges "largely as a result of his own actions" or as a result of "political abuse of the justice system." The results were not close[41]: by a six-to-one margin, self-identified Republican voters agreed with the latter, convinced that corrupt and nefarious forces had conspired against the former president.

Among GOP voters, there was a consensus: Trump's prosecutions were not a consequence of his own alleged misconduct. The party's devotees had heard the rewritten story, and they liked it far more than reality.

The propaganda campaign, in other words, had achieved its intended goal. It was the kind of success the party had seen too many times before.

In George Orwell's classic dystopian novel, *1984*, the story's protagonist, Winston Smith, works for a powerful agency known as the Ministry of Truth, which is responsible for overseeing the ruling party's propaganda. The hero disapproves of the ministry's expectations, but as the story's perpetual war continues, he rewrites history in order to satisfy the ruling party's demands.

"The party told you to reject the evidence of your eyes and ears," Orwell wrote. "It was their final, most essential command."

It's a principle the contemporary Republican Party has embraced with far too much vigor, indifferent to the fact that Orwell's story was a cautionary tale. Indeed, when Trump told supporters in 2018, "What you're seeing and what you're reading is not what's happening," it didn't take long for observers to note that the presidential phrasing could've been scripted by Orwell himself.[42]

Efforts to rewrite recent history have become a scourge on the polity. They have a fundamentally transgressive effect on the public discourse. They are intended to leave the public misinformed, confused, and disoriented about the critically important events of their civil society.

But just as important are the practical implications: these are dangerous authoritarian tactics that contribute to the weakening of democracy.

In 1967, political theorist Hannah Arendt condemned the practice of "organized lying," explaining that it erodes political systems from within. The integrity of the truth, she wrote, "is the ground on which we stand and the sky that stretches above us."[43]

To replace accurate versions of reality with deceptive counternarratives is to weaken our collective foundation and pollute the air overhead with toxic nonsense.

In the aftermath of the January 6 attack on the U.S. Capitol, as Republicans set out to rewrite the story of the insurrectionist violence, Andrew Gawthorpe, a historian at Leiden University in the Netherlands, added, "The inability to reach a shared understanding of recent history poses a grave danger. While political parties and factions will always disagree over how to interpret the world and its history, the give-and-take and trust which are vital to the functioning of democratic politics depend on a common baseline understanding of reality."[44]

Gawthorpe went on to argue that if a political party simply refuses to accept those terms, "it is signaling that it is capable of doing almost anything to gain the power necessary to remake the world in the shadow of its lies."

Increasingly overt GOP hostility toward democracy is multifaceted and takes a variety of forms. Republicans at the national level, for example, are reflexively skeptical of election results that disappoint them. They have few qualms about erecting new barriers between voters and ballot boxes.

They identify institutions that undergird our politics—a free press, the rule of law, civil rights guarantees, et al.—and degrade them with partisan ire.

But the Republicans' war on the recent past is a sizable piece of the same appalling mosaic. Its combatants believe that their failures, scandals, and embarrassments need not be addressed because the truth need not be tolerated. The public's understanding of the events is little more than malleable clay to be reshaped into the GOP's preferred image.

If there were an easy solution that would end the conflict, it would be eagerly presented here. No such simple fix exists, though those who care about the integrity of recent history—from voters to educators to journalists—have an obvious role to play in taking an unyielding stance in support of the truth, which needs champions, because it's not enough to let it speak for itself.

But just as notable is the fact that recognizing misinformation campaigns is a key element of defeating them. To understand the Republican Party's propaganda campaigns is to help strip them of their potency.

Like a magic trick that becomes less impressive after an audience knows how it's done, voters are less likely to believe rewritten stories once they're exposed as part of a pathological sham. With this in mind, this book is intended to pull back the curtain, effectively inoculating readers from would-be illusionists trying to undermine their democracy through rhetorical sleights of hand.

When GOP voices tell voters not to believe their lying eyes, using a combination of shameless dishonesty, partisan coordination, and relentless repetition, the rhetorical strategy is predicated on the idea that they can safely get away with it. History tells us, however, that parties change their tactics when an electorate tells them they must.

As the American experiment confronts new perils, the time for the Republican Party to hear such a message is now. Time will tell whether voters are willing to send that message or will instead continue to allow the party to lead us further into our own partisan version of Orwell's forever war.

ACKNOWLEDGMENTS

My most sincere thanks to Peter Hubbard, Jessica Vestuto, and the amazing team at HarperCollins, who are a joy to work with. Thanks also to the incredible Laurie Liss and her terrific colleagues at Sterling Lord Literistic, who encouraged me at just the right time, and in just the right way.

My gratitude remains endless for my friend and hero Rachel Maddow, who hopefully knows how much I appreciate the incredible generosity she's shown me over many years. Thanks also to the rest of my MSNBC family, including Cory Gnazzo, Laura Conaway, Will Femia, Matthew Alexander, Lisa Rubin, and Alex Wagner.

I would be lost without the support of my friends, neighbors, and family members. A special thanks to Michael Weitzner, Zoe Poulson, Rob Boston, Alex Woolfson, Bill Simmon,

Emily Stoneking, Virginia Simmon, Frederick Buckland, Bill Wolff, and E. J. Dionne for their encouragement.

Finally, and most important, my deepest thanks to my mom, Gini, who caught a few more typos in my early drafts than I'd like to admit, and my wife, Eve, who remembers me saying I only intended to write one book, but who extended bighearted encouragement as I wrote a second.

NOTES

INTRODUCTION: **"WITH TIME, PEOPLE FORGET"**

1   Carl Hulse, "Six Takeaways from Cassidy Hutchinson's Explosive Testimony," *New York Times*, June 28, 2022.

2   Steve Benen, "'60 Minutes' Bothers Trump with the Truth About the Economy," MSNBC online, last modified October 22, 2020.

3   Linda Qiu, "In Farewell Video, Trump Repeats Familiar Falsehoods," *New York Times*, January 19, 2021.

4   Hope Yen and Calvin Woodward, "AP Fact Check: Trump Takes Credit for Obama's Gains for Vets," Associated Press, May 28, 2019.

5   Joe Davidson, "U.S. International Image Rebounds with Biden Reversing Trump Policies," *Washington Post*, August 11, 2023.

6   Daniel Dale, "The 15 Most Notable Lies of Donald Trump's Presidency," CNN online, last modified January 16, 2021.

7   Aaron Blake, "Most Republicans Say Trump Didn't Even Try to Overturn the Election," *Washington Post*, October 26, 2023.

8   Jonathan Weisman, "I.R.S. Scrutiny Went Beyond the Political," *New York Times*, July 4, 2013.

9   Steve Benen, "So Long, IRS 'Scandal,'" MSNBC online, last modified January 14, 2014.

10 Timothy M. Phelps, "Justice Dept. Won't File Criminal Charges over Allegations of IRS Targeting Conservative Groups," *Los Angeles Times*, October 23, 2015.

11 Emma Dumain, "House GOP Threatens Contempt Vote for IRS Head," *Roll Call*, July 27, 2015.

12 Rachel Bade, "IRS Impeachment Leader Under Fire over Fundraising," *Politico*, May 24, 2016.

13 Kate Riga, "In GOP Opposition to Beefing Up IRS Enforcement, Shades of a Fake, Obama-Era Zombie Scandal," Talking Points Memo, July 20, 2021.

14 Jeff Stein, Tony Room, and Yeganeh Torbati, "Conservative Groups Mount Opposition to Increase in IRS Budget, Threatening White House Infrastructure Plan," *Washington Post*, July 8, 2021.

15 William McGurn, "Defund Joe Biden's IRS," *Wall Street Journal*, July 5, 2021.

16 Steve Benen, "McCarthy Tries to Revive Interest in a Faux Controversy from 2013," MSNBC online, December 8, 2022.

17 Phil McCausland, "With No Evidence, Trump Claims 'Millions' Voted Illegally," NBC News online, last modified November 28, 2016.

18 Kasie Hunt, "Trump Again Makes Debunked Claim: 'Illegals' Cost Me Popular Vote," NBC News online, last modified January 24, 2017.

19 Philip Bump, "Reminder: In an Anti-recount Filing, Trump's Lawyers Said the Election Was 'Not Tainted by Fraud or Mistake,'" *Washington Post*, January 25, 2017.

20 Glenn Thrush, "Trump's Voter Fraud Example? A Troubled Tale With Bernhard Langer," *New York Times*, January 25, 2017.

21 Thrush, "Trump's Voter Fraud Example?"

22 Karen Tumulty and Juliet Eilperin, "Trump Pressured Park Service to Find Proof for His Claims About Inauguration Crowd," *Washington Post*, January 26, 2017.

23 Megan Garber, "The First Lie of the Trump Presidency," *The Atlantic*, January 13, 2019.

24 Glenn Kessler, "Spicer Earns Four Pinocchios for False Claims on Inauguration Crowd Size," *Washington Post*, January 22, 2017.

25 Jessica Taylor, "Sean Spicer Praises Successor Sanders: 'She Understands What the President Wants,'" NPR, July 18, 2018.

26 Phil Helsel, Ariana Brockington, and Marianna Sotomayor, "Trump Takes Heat for Blaming Charlottesville Violence on 'Many Sides,'" NBC News online, last updated August 12, 2017.

27 Rosie Gray, "Trump Defends White-Nationalist Protesters: 'Some Very Fine People on Both Sides,'" *The Atlantic*, August 15, 2017.

28 Emily Kopp, "Trump 'Always Said That He Hated Losers. Robert E. Lee Was a Loser,' Rep. James Clyburn says," *Roll Call*, April 29, 2019.

29 Aaron Blake, "Pence Joins in the Effort to Rewrite Trump's Charlottesville History," *Washington Post*, October 8, 2020.

30 Steve Benen, "Short on Friends, Trump's White House Councils Start to Unravel," MSNBC online, August 18, 2017.

31 Christina Caron, "More Charities Cancel Fund-Raisers at Trump's Mar-a-Lago Club," *New York Times*, August 20, 2017.

32 Nicole Gaudiano, "Trump Creates 1776 Commission to Promote 'Patriotic Education,'" *Politico*, November 2, 2020.

33 Alana Wise, "Trump Announces 'Patriotic Education' Commission, a Largely Political Move," NPR online, September 17, 2020.

34 Jennifer Schuessler, "The Ideas Behind Trump's 1776 Commission Report," *New York Times*, January 19, 2021.

35 Michael Crowley and Jennifer Schuessler, "Trump's 1776 Commission Critiques Liberalism in Report Derided by Historians," *New York Times*, January 18, 2021.

36 Solcyre Burga, "Florida Approves Controversial Guidelines for Black History Curriculum. Here's What to Know," *Time*, July 20, 2023.

37 Kevin Kruse, "Standard Issue," Campaign Trails, Substack newsletter, July 22, 2023.

38 Jamelle Bouie, "Ron DeSantis and the State Where History Goes to Die," *New York Times*, July 28, 2023.

39 Ana Ceballos, "Florida's Conservative PragerU Teaching Texts Labeled 'Indoctrination,'" *Tampa Bay Times*, August 4, 2023.

40 Sophie Lawton, John Knefel, and Jacina Hollins-Borges, "Research File: We Watched Every PragerU Kids Video. Here Are the Lowlights," Media Matters online, September 8, 2023.

41 Mahita Gajanan, "Kellyanne Conway Defends White House's Falsehoods as 'Alternative Facts,'" *Time*, January 22, 2017.

42 Emily Birnbaum, "Trump Says 'Polls Are Fake' Before Bragging About Poll Showing His Popularity," *The Hill*, July 31, 2018.

43 Rebecca Morin and David Cohen, "Giuliani: 'Truth Isn't Truth,'" *Politico*, last updated August 19, 2018.

44 Aaron Blake, "'Facts Develop': The Trump Team's New 'Alternative Facts'-esque Ways to Explain Its Falsehoods," *Washington Post*, August 6, 2018.

45 William Cummings, "Rudy Giuliani Says Trump Is 'Honest' Because Facts Are 'in the Eye of the Beholder,'" *USA Today*, August 15, 2018.

46 Lili Loofbourow, "The Moment That Should Have Changed Everything," Slate, October 7, 2020.

47 Billy Bush, "Yes, Donald Trump, You Said That," *New York Times*, December 3, 2017.

48 Donald Trump (@realDonaldTrump), "With TIME, people forget! All of these Indictments and Lawsuits against me were started by Crooked Joe Biden and his Radical Left Fascists. It is their weapon of choice in the upcoming 2024 Presidential Election. They feel, for a fact, that Republican leadership isn't tough enough to stop them, or do anything about their abuse and fraud. But I'll stop them, because we have No Choice—If we don't WIN, WE WILL HAVE A COUNTRY NO LONGER!!!" Truth Social, August 25, 2023, 7:30 p.m.

49 Max Boot, "Republicans Are Rewriting the Past So They Can Seize Power in the Future," *Washington Post*, July 15, 2021.

CHAPTER 1: **"RUSSIA, RUSSIA, RUSSIA"**

1   Rob Crilly, "Top Republican Calls Mar-a-Lago Raid 'Russia Hoax 2.0,'" *Daily Mail*, August 31, 2022.

2   Herb Scribner, "Trump Allies Back Former President amid Indictment Speculation," Axios, March 18, 2023.

3   Molly Ball, "Trump's Indictment Drama Showcased His Rivals' Weakness," *Time*, March 30, 2023.

4   Maggie Astor, "Trump's Call for 'Termination' of Constitution Draws Rebukes," *New York Times*, December 4, 2022.

5   Olivia Olander, "Trump Denies He Suggested 'Termination' of Constitution, Without Deleting Post," *Politico*, December 5, 2022.

6   Graham Kates, "Trump Sues N.Y. Attorney General Letitia James, Seeking to End Investigation," CBS News online, December 21, 2021.

7   Brad Dress, "Trump Calls Jan. 6 Panel Members 'Thugs and Scoundrels' Ahead of Monday Hearing," *The Hill*, December 18, 2022.

8   Jared Gans, "Trump Rages over Legal Problems on Truth Social," *The Hill*, July 24, 2023.

9   Nick Gass, "Trump on Putin's Alleged Killing of Journalists: 'At Least He's a Leader,'" *Politico*, December 18, 2015.

10 Kate Sullivan, "Trump Signed Letter of Intent for Trump Tower Moscow Project Despite Giuliani Insisting He Didn't," CNN, December 19, 2018.

11 Steve Benen, "Giuliani Proven Wrong About Trump Tower Moscow Letter of Intent," MSNBC online, last updated December 19, 2018.

12 Matthew Zeitlin, "Trump Denied Having Any Business Dealings with Russia a Bunch of Times," Slate, November 29, 2018.

13 Jonathan Chait, "Why Is Donald Trump a Patsy for Vladimir Putin?" *New York*, April 28, 2016.

14 Michael Crowley, "The Kremlin's Candidate," *Politico*, May–June 2016.

15 Ellen Nakashima, "Russian Government Hackers Penetrated DNC, Stole Opposition Research on Trump," *Washington Post*, June 14, 2016.

16 Steve Benen, "Trump's Indifference to Russia's Election Attack Raises Alarm," MSNBC online, June 15, 2017.

17 Elizabeth Weise, "Tech Crowd Goes Wild for Trump's '400-Pound Hacker,'" *USA Today*, September 27, 2016.

18 Robert Windrem and William M. Arkin, "Trump Told Russia to Blame for Hacks Long Before 2016 Debate," NBC News online, last updated October 10, 2016.

19 Erica R. Hendry, "Trump Asked Russia to Find Clinton's Emails. On or Around the Same Day, Russians Targeted Her Accounts," PBS online, July 13, 2018.

20 Hendry, "Trump Asked Russia to Find Clinton's Emails."

21 Max Fisher, "Donald Trump's Appeal to Russia Shocks Foreign Policy Experts," *New York Times*, July 28, 2016.

22 Nahal Toosi and Seung Min Kim, "'Treason'? Critics Savage Trump over Russia Hack Comments," *Politico*, July 27, 2016.

23 Andrew Kaczynski and Christopher Massie, "Former Bush NSA, CIA Chief Slams Trump's Russia Comments," BuzzFeed, July 27, 2016.

24 Eliza Collins, "Yes, 17 Intelligence Agencies Really Did Say Russia Was Behind Hacking," *USA Today*, last updated December 16, 2016.

25 Josh Marshall, "Mind-Boggling," Talking Points Memo, January 6, 2017.

26 Michael S. Schmidt, Matthew Rosenberg, Adam Goldman, and Matt Apuzzo, "Intercepted Russian Communications Part of Inquiry into Trump Associates," *New York Times*, January 19, 2017.

27 Jamie Gangel, Jeremy Herb, and Elizabeth Stuart, "Trump Said He Knew Coronavirus Was 'Deadly Stuff' Early in Pandemic According to New Woodward Book," CNN online, September 9, 2020.

28 Michal Kranz, "'He Has Something to Fear': Former CIA Director John Brennan Says Russia 'May Have Something' Damaging on Trump," Business Insider, March 21, 2018.

29 Jonathan Swan and Mike Allen, "Trump's Helsinki Humiliation," Axios, July 16, 2018.

30 Matthew Rosenberg, "U.S. Intelligence Community Reacts with Fury to Trump's Rebuke," *New York Times*, July 16, 2018.

31 Dartunorro Clark, "'Shameful,' 'Treasonous,' 'Disgraceful': Trump Slammed from All Sides for News Conference with Putin," NBC News online, last updated July 16, 2018.

32 Jonathan Swan and Mike Allen, "Trump Officials Embarrassed by Putin Show," Axios, July 17, 2018.

33 Tiff Fehr, Troy Griggs, Jasmine C. Lee, Jaymin Patel, Rumsey Taylor, and Josh Williams, "Read Attorney General William Barr's Summary of the Mueller Report," *New York Times*, March 24, 2019.

34 Eric Tucker, "Judge Sharply Rebukes Barr's Handling of Mueller Report," Associated Press, March 5, 2020.

35 Steve Benen, "The Problem with Trump's 'No Obstruction' Claim: It's Plainly False," MSNBC online, last updated April 22, 2019.

36 Matt Apuzzo and Adam Goldman, "The Mueller Report Is 448 Pages Long. You Need to Know These 7 Key Things," *New York Times*, May 20, 2020.

37 Aaron Blake, "5 Persistent Myths About the Mueller Report," *Washington Post*, April 27, 2019.

38 "10 Episodes Where Trump Might Have Obstructed Justice," *Politico*, April 18, 2019.

39 Aaron Blake, "Mueller Was Right to Worry About William Barr's Actions, a New Poll Suggests," *Washington Post*, May 2, 2019.

40 Hope Yen and Calvin Woodward, "AP Fact Check: Trump, Putin on 'No Collusion'; Economy Myths," Associated Press, May 6, 2019.

41 Philip Bump, "Trump Claims Russia's Outreach Was 'Rebuffed at Every Turn,' Which Is the Opposite of True," *Washington Post*, May 3, 2019.

42 Ken Dilanian, "Trump Says He Didn't Discuss Hacked Emails with Roger Stone. A Bipartisan Senate Report Says He Did," NBC News online, August 18, 2020.

43 Sue Halpern, "Why Would Paul Manafort Share Polling Data with Russia?" *The New Yorker*, January 10, 2019.

44 Steve Benen, "Trump's Dubious Pitch: Russian Interference Was Inconsequential," MSNBC online, last updated February 19, 2018.

45 Adam Entous, Ellen Nakashima, and Greg Miller, "Secret CIA Assessment Says Russia Was Trying to Help Trump Win White House," *Washington Post*, December 9, 2016.

46 The Mueller report read, "In evaluating whether evidence about collective action of multiple individuals constituted a crime, we applied the framework of conspiracy law, not the concept of 'collusion.' . . . Like collusion, 'coordination' does not have a settled definition in federal criminal law."

47 Mark Sherman, "The 10 Instances of Possible Obstruction in Mueller Report," Associated Press, April 18, 2019.

48 Eric Tucker, Mary Clare Jalonick, and Michael Balsamo, "Mueller: I Did Not Clear Trump of Obstruction of Justice," PBS online, July 24, 2019.

49 Emily Schultheis, "Mike Pence Says Trump Adviser's Contact with Russia Was 'Strictly Coincidental,'" CBS News online, January 15, 2017.

50 Jake Miller, "Flashback: Top Trump Aide 'Absolutely' Denies Campaign Contact with Russia," CBS News online, January 11, 2017.

51 David Morgan, "Trump Team Collusion with Russia an 'Open Question,' Says Clinton Aide," Reuters, December 18, 2016.

52 Rosalind S. Helderman, Tom Hamburger, and Carol D. Leonnig, "Russians Interacted with At Least 14 Trump Associates During the Campaign and Transition," *Washington Post*, December 9, 2018.

53 Abigail Abrams, "The Attorney General Said There Was 'No Collusion.' But Trump Associates Still Interacted with Russians More Than 100 Times," *Time*, April 18, 2019.

54 Chuck Rosenberg, "Michael Flynn Lied to the FBI and That Lie Was a Crime—White House and Alan Dershowitz Objections Ignore the Facts," NBC News online, December 20, 2018.

55 Andrew Prokop, "All of Robert Mueller's Indictments and Plea Deals in the Russia Investigation," Vox, December 17, 2019.

56 Adam Edelman, Julia Ainsley, Ken Dilanian, and Tom Winter, "Special Counsel Mueller Indicts 13 Russians with Interfering in 2016 U.S. Election," NBC News online, last updated February 17, 2018.

57 Jonathan Chait, "Trump Now Rewriting History to Deny Russia Wanted Him to Win," *New York*, May 14, 2020.

58 Press Release, "2018 Pulitzer Prizes," Pulitzer Prize Board, April 16, 2018.

59 Kevin Breuninger, "Pulitzer Board Rejects Trump's Calls to Revoke Prizes for Reporting on Russian Election Meddling," CNBC online, last updated July 18, 2022.

60 Jan Wolfe and Jonathan Stempel, "Donald Trump Sues Hillary Clinton over 2016 Russian Collusion Allegations," Reuters, March 25, 2022.

61 Aaron Blake, "Trump's Lawsuit Against Clinton and 47 Others Is a Predictable Mess," *Washington Post*, March 24, 2022.

62 Erin Doherty, "Judge Throws Out Trump's Lawsuit Against Hillary Clinton," Axios, September 9, 2022.

63 Kevin Breuninger, "Judge Sanctions Trump Lawyers over 'Frivolous' Collusion Lawsuit Against Clinton, DNC," CNBC online, last updated November 10, 2022.

64 Zoë Richards, "Judge Sanctions Trump and His Lawyer Nearly $1 Million for 'Frivolous' Lawsuit Targeting Hillary Clinton," NBC News, January 19, 2023.

65 House Judiciary GOP (@JudiciaryGOP), "They all lied to you," Twitter, June 21, 2023, 9:15 a.m.

66 Philip Bump, "House Republicans Want to Remind You That Russia Helped Trump in 2016," *Washington Post*, June 21, 2023.

67 Timothy Snyder (@TimothyDSnyder), "Moscow worked hard to get Trump elected in 2016. Choosing not to know that is choosing not to care about political reality and national security," Twitter, June 22, 2023, 1:07 p.m.

68 Steve Benen, "The Most Important Flaw in Rubio's Woeful New Trump Defense," MSNBC online, August 3, 2023.

69 Alexander Mallin and Soo Rin Kim, "DOJ Watchdog Finds Russia Investigation Not Improper, Despite Missteps," ABC News online, December 9, 2019.

70 Charlie Savage, "After Years of Political Hype, the Durham Inquiry Failed to Deliver," *New York Times*, May 17, 2023.

71 Carrie Johnson, "Special Counsel Durham Fails First Courtroom Test in His Three-Year Probe," NPR online, May 31, 2022.

72 Eric Lutz, "John Durham Spent Four Years Trying to Uncover an Anti-Trump Witch Hunt and He Got Nothing," *Vanity Fair*, May 16, 2023.

73 Lutz, "John Durham Spent Four Years."

74 Marsha Blackburn (@MarshaBlackburn), "The Russian hoax was a figment of Hillary Clinton's imagination," Twitter, May 15, 2023, 9:12 p.m.

75 Ted Cruz (@tedcruz), "Disgraceful. Obama-Biden officials and the corrupt corporate media pushed these piles of lies for years. Accountability now—starting with WaPo and The New York Times returning their Pulitzer Prizes for breathlessly spreading these 'Russia, Russia, Russia' lies," Twitter, May 15, 2023, 7:03 p.m.

76 Eric Schmitt (@Eric_Schmitt), "The findings of the Durham report confirmed what many of us already knew—the Trump 'collusion' story and probe were politically motivated hit jobs. The FBI has a lot of questions to answer in the coming days and months," Twitter, May 15, 2023, 6:17 p.m.

77 Josh Hawley (@HawleyMO), "It was all a hoax," Twitter, May 15, 2023, 4:16 p.m.

78 William Thornton, "Tuberville on Durham Report: 'If People Don't Go to Jail . . . Let's Don't Have Elections Anymore,'" AL.com, last updated May 16, 2023.

79 Susan Ferrechio, "No Remorse: Democrats Stick to Trump-Russia Collusion Claims Despite Durham Report," *Washington Times*, May 16, 2023.

80 Donald Trump (@realDonaldTrump), video excerpt, Truth Social, May 16, 2023, 10:17 p.m.

81 Jonathan Chait, "John Durham Admits He Knows Little About Russia Scandal," *New York*, June 21, 2023.

82 Steve Benen, "Despite Reality, Trump Pretends the Durham Report Wasn't a Dud," MSNBC online, May 16, 2023.

83 Jonathan Weisman, "The Durham Report Offered Few Conclusions. The Right Drew Its Own," *New York Times*, May 16, 2023.

84 "6 Months In, a Record Low for Trump, with Troubles from Russia to Health Care," ABC News online, July 16, 2017.

85 "84% of U.S. Voters Want to See Mueller Report, Quinnipiac University National Poll Finds; Dems Divided on Support for Israelis or Palestinians," Quinnipiac University, March 26, 2019.

86   Philip Bump, "House Republicans Want to Remind You That Russia Helped Trump in 2016."

87   Jason Daley, "How Adlai Stevenson Stopped Russian Interference in the 1960 Election," *Smithsonian Magazine*, January 4, 2017.

88   "Russia Has Often Tried to Influence Elections, with Little Success," *The Economist*, December 17, 2016.

89   David Corn, "Dana Rohrabacher Says Anyone 'in This Town' Would Meet with Russians Peddling Political Dirt," *Mother Jones*, July 30, 2018.

90   Hope Yen, "Giuliani: Nothing Wrong with Trump Camp Taking Russian Help," Associated Press, April 21, 2019.

91   Justin Doom and Kelly Terez, "Trump Says 'I Think I'd Take' Help If Foreigners Offered Dirt on Political Opponents," ABC News online, June 13, 2019.

CHAPTER 2: **"INCREASINGLY DETACHED FROM REALITY"**

1   Josh Dawsey, "Trump Campaign Paid Researchers to Prove 2020 Fraud but Kept Findings Secret," *Washington Post*, February 11, 2023.

2   Dawsey, "Trump Campaign Paid Researchers to Prove 2020 Fraud."

3   Josh Dawsey, "A Second Firm Hired by Trump Campaign Found No Evidence of Election Fraud," *Washington Post*, April 27, 2023.

4   Sarah D. Wire, "Trump Was Repeatedly Told Election Fraud Claims Were False," *Los Angeles Times*, June 13, 2022.

5   Meridith McGraw, "Trump's Election Fraud Claims Were False. Here Are His Advisers Who Said So," *Politico*, June 13, 2022.

6   Lisa Mascaro and Eric Tucker, "1/6 Panel: Told Repeatedly He Lost, Trump Refused to Go," Associated Press, June 10, 2022.

7   Daniel Dale, "Fact Check: 10 of the Lies Trump Used to Try to Overturn His Georgia Defeat," CNN online, August 14, 2023.

8   Steve Benen, "Trump Fires 'One of the Heroes' of 2020 for Telling the Truth," MSNBC online, November 18, 2020.

9   Alex Seitz-Wald, "'Detached from Reality': Trump Insiders Worked to Convince Him He Lost," NBC News online, last updated June 13, 2022.

10   Katie Benner, "Trump's Attorney General Said the President Showed No Interest in 'Actual Facts,'" *New York Times*, June 13, 2022.

11   Michael D. Shear and Zolan Kanno-Youngs, "In Arizona, Trump Boasts About His Wall and Repeats Unfounded Predictions of Voter Fraud," *New York Times*, June 23, 2020.

12   Sanya Mansoor, "'I Have to See.' President Trump Refuses to Say If He Will Accept the 2020 Election Results," *Time*, July 19, 2020.

13   Linda Qiu, "Barr Repeats Trump Falsehoods in Congressional Testimony," *New York Times*, July 29, 2020.

14 Alex Marquardt, Pamela Brown, and Manu Raju, "Trump's Own Intelligence Officials Contradict His Repeated Claims of Mail-In Voting Fraud," CNN online, last updated July 31, 2020.

15 Amy Gardner, "Election Officials Contradict Barr's Assertion That Counterfeit Mail Ballots Produced by a Foreign Country Are a 'Real' Worry," *Washington Post*, June 2, 2020.

16 John Kass, "AG Bill Barr Says Federal Corruption Hunters Never 'at a Loss for Work' in Chicago," *Chicago Tribune*, September 11, 2020.

17 Jerry Lambe, "Bill Barr Pushes 'Wild' and 'Fanciful' Felonious Postman Hypothetical, Says Liberals Are the Ones Projecting 'Bullsh*t,'" Law & Crime, September 15, 2020.

18 Salvador Rizzo, "Trump's Fusillade of Falsehoods on Mail Voting," *Washington Post*, September 11, 2020.

19 Dan Coats, "What's at Stake in This Election? The American Democratic Experiment," *New York Times*, September 17, 2020.

20 Steve Benen, "With Early Voting Poised to Begin, Trump's Voting Lies Intensify," MSNBC online, September 14, 2020.

21 Jonathan Swan, "Scoop: Trump's Plan to Declare Premature Victory," Axios, last updated November 1, 2020.

22 Annie Karni, "With No Winner in the Presidential Race, Trump Falsely Asserts That He Has Prevailed," *New York Times*, November 4, 2020.

23 Karni, "With No Winner in the Presidential Race."

24 Jonathan Chait, "Trump Says Vote-Counting Should Only Continue in States Where He's Behind," *New York*, November 4, 2020.

25 Lisa Lerer, "Trump's Stunning News Conference," *New York Times*, November 5, 2020.

26 Ezra Klein (@ezraklein), "But what we're seeing is the sitting President of the United States using the power of his office, his megaphone, and his supporters, to try to stop the votes against him from being counted. Not a drill, a joke, a hypothetical. It's happening," Twitter, November 5, 2020, 11:05 a.m.

27 Bess Levin, "Kevin McCarthy, Shameless Hack, Claims He Never Supported Trump's Effort to Overturn the Election," *Vanity Fair*, March 19, 2021.

28 Aaron Rupar, "Key Republicans Quickly Fall in Line Behind Trump's Attempt to Undermine the Election," Vox, November 6, 2020.

29 Ashley Parker and Philip Rucker, "Republicans Echo Trump's Baseless Election Claims, Undermining Biden's Transition," *Washington Post*, November 10, 2020.

30 Tim Alberta (@TimAlberta), "Let's be clear about something. We don't yet have any evidence proving voter fraud was committed in this election. We do have evidence that Republicans—from the president to congressional leaders to the party chair and her aides—are lying to the public," Twitter, November 6, 2020, 10:17 p.m.

31 Tim Alberta, "The Election That Broke the Republican Party," *Politico*, last updated November 7, 2020.

32 Chris Murphy, United States senator for Connecticut, "Murphy: The President and Congressional Republicans' Refusal to Accept the Free and Fair Election Results Is an Assault on Our Democracy," press release, November 11, 2020.

33 Peter Baker and Lara Jakes, "Fighting Election Results, Trump Employs a New Weapon: The Government," *New York Times*, November 10, 2020.

34 Thomas B. Edsall, "What Is Trump Playing At?" *New York Times*, November 11, 2020.

35 Steve Benen, "Trump Lawyers Face Tough Questions over Ridiculous Election Suit," MSNBC online, July 13, 2021.

36 Maggie Haberman, "Trump Floats Improbable Survival Scenarios as He Ponders His Future," *New York Times*, November 12, 2020.

37 Emma Platoff, "In New Lawsuit, Texas Contests Election Results in Georgia, Wisconsin, Michigan, Pennsylvania," *Texas Tribune*, last updated December 9, 2020.

38 Brad Heath (@bradheath), "So Texas' Attorney General is literally asking the Supreme Court to throw out the results of other states' presidential elections, set aside the millions of votes cast in states that are not Texas and have other state legislatures make Trump president," Twitter, December 8, 2020, 10:18 a.m.

39 Tierney Sneed, "In Bonkers SCOTUS Bid, Texas Tries to Sue to Overturn WI, PA, GA and MI Election Results," Talking Points Memo, December 8, 2020.

40 Chris Hayes (@chrislhayes), "Like so much of what's happened over the last month the Texas lawsuit is both laughably buffoonish and just unspeakably poisonous in what it represents," Twitter, December 9, 2020, 3:33 p.m.

41 Pete Williams and Dartunorro Clark, "Supreme Court Rejects Texas' Effort to Overturn Election in Fatal Blow to Trump Legal Blitz to Stop Biden," NBC News online, last updated December 12, 2020.

42 "House Members Who Signed a Brief Asking the Supreme Court to Consider Overturning the Election," ProPublica, December 10, 2020.

43 David A. Graham, "The GOP Abandons Democracy," *The Atlantic*, December 10, 2020.

44 Jane C. Timm, "Rudy Giuliani Baselessly Alleges 'Centralized' Voter Fraud at Free-Wheeling News Conference," NBC News online, last updated December 19, 2020.

45 Alana Wise, "Trump Fires Election Security Director Who Corrected Voter Fraud Disinformation," NPR online, November 17, 2020.

46 Pam Fessler, "Despite More Than 2 Dozen Legal Losses, Trump's Lawyers Press On with Election Fights," NPR online, November 19, 2020.

47   Josh Wingrove, "Trump Slams Detroit, Wayne County While Criticizing Election Results," *Detroit News*, last updated November 27, 2020.

48   Aamer Madhani and Kevin Freking, "In Video, Trump Recycles Unsubstantiated Voter Fraud Claims," Associated Press, December 2, 2020.

49   Taegan Goddard, "Trump Says Election Challenges 'Not Over,'" Political Wire, December 13, 2020.

50   Donald Trump (@realDonaldTrump), "I WON THE ELECTION IN A LANDSLIDE, but remember, I only think in terms of legal votes, not all of the fake voters and fraud that miraculously floated in from everywhere! What a disgrace!" Twitter, December 12, 2020, 8:05 a.m.

51   Grace Segers, "Trump Makes Multiple False Claims in First Campaign Rally Since Election Loss," CBS News online, December 6, 2020.

52   Steve Benen, "The Problem(s) with Trump's Pushback Against the Jan. 6 Probe," MSNBC online, June 14, 2022.

53   Philip Bump, "Trump Drops 12-Page, Greatest-Hits Collection of His False Fraud Claims," *Washington Post*, June 14, 2022.

54   Kierra Frazier, "Trump Says He Plans to Hold Press Conference Responding to Georgia Indictment," *Politico*, August 15, 2023.

55   Maggie Haberman and Jonathan Swan, "Trump Plans to Release 100-Page Report on Georgia Election Fraud Claims," *New York Times*, August 15, 2023.

56   Vaughn Hillyard and Garrett Haake, "Trump Scraps Plans to Release 'Irrefutable Report' Claiming Election Fraud in Georgia," NBC News online, August 17, 2023.

57   Katherine Faulders and Jonathan Karl, "Trump's Legal Advisers Urge Him to Cancel Press Conference to Refute Georgia Allegations: Sources," ABC News online, August 17, 2023.

58   Barbara Sprunt, "Here's What the Jan. 6 Panel's References to '2,000 Mules' Is About," NPR online, June 13, 2022.

59   Danny Hakim and Alexandra Berzon, "A Big Lie in a New Package," *New York Times*, May 29, 2022.

60   Ali Swenson, "FACT FOCUS: Gaping Holes in the Claim of 2K Ballot 'Mules,'" Associated Press, May 3, 2022.

61   Philip Bump, "The Dishonest Pivot at the Heart of the New Voter-Fraud Conspiracy," *Washington Post*, April 29, 2022.

62   Philip Bump, "Even the Geolocation Maps in '2000 Mules' Are Misleading," *Washington Post*, last updated May 19, 2022.

63   Anthony L. Fisher, "Dinesh D'Souza's Vile Big Lie Documentary Is Too Stupid Even for Fox," Daily Beast, May 19, 2022.

64   Amanda Carpenter, "Dinesh D'Souza's *2000 Mules* Is a Hilarious Mockumentary," The Bulwark, May 17, 2022.

65   Ja'han Jones, "Right-Wing Group Behind '2000 Mules' Could Face Federal Scrutiny," MSNBC online, October 17, 2022.

66 Zachary Petrizzo, "Bill Barr Outright Cackles at Dinesh D'Souza's Nutty '2000 Mules' Movie," Daily Beast, last updated June 13, 2022.

67 Ewan Palmer, "Donald Trump Holds Screening of '2,000 Mules' Documentary at Mar-a-Lago," Newsweek, May 5, 2022.

68 Steve Benen, "GOP's Biggs, Colleagues Seek Hearing on Claims from Debunked Film," MSNBC online, July 14, 2022.

69 Bryan Schott, "Sen. Mike Lee Embraces Baseless Claims About Election Fraud in the 2020 Election," Salt Lake Tribune, last updated June 10, 2022.

70 Benen, "The Problem(s) with Trump's Pushback Against the Jan. 6 Probe."

71 Caitlin Oprysko, "Trump Says He'll Leave Office Peacefully If He Loses in November," Politico, June 12, 2020.

72 Karen Yourish, Larry Buchanan, and Denise Lu, "The 147 Republicans Who Voted to Overturn Election Results," New York Times, January 7, 2021.

73 Kevin Collier and Jane C. Timm, "In Private, Fox News Stars and Staffers Blasted Election Fraud Claims as Bogus, Court Filing Shows," NBC News online, last updated February 17, 2023.

74 "More Americans Happy About Trump Loss Than Biden Win," Monmouth University Polling Institute, November 18, 2020.

75 Jennifer Agiesta and Ariel Edwards-Levy, "CNN Poll: Percentage of Republicans Who Think Biden's 2020 Win Was Illegitimate Ticks Back Up Near 70%," CNN, August 3, 2023.

76 Ted Cruz, United States Senator for Texas, "Joint Statement from Senators Cruz, Johnson, Lankford, Daines, Kennedy, Blackburn, Braun, Senators-Elect Lummis, Marshall, Hagerty, Tuberville," press release, January 2, 2021.

77 Jordain Carney, "GOP Senator Won't Rule Out Challenging Electoral College Results in Congress," The Hill, December 9, 2020.

78 Susan Glasser (@sbg1), "This is a big red flashing light of trouble for American democracy," Twitter, April 30, 2021, 2:21 p.m.

79 "Voting Laws Roundup: October 2021," Brennan Center for Justice at NYU Law, October 4, 2021.

80 Gary Fields, Anthony Izaguirre, and Sudhin Thanawala, "New State Voter Fraud Units Finding Few Cases from Midterms," Associated Press, November 26, 2022.

81 Charlie Crist, "Don't Let DeSantis' Election Police Intimidate You into Not Voting," South Florida Sun Sentinel, September 13, 2022.

82 Daniel Dale, "Trump and Other Republicans Are Already Casting Doubt on Midterm Results," CNN online, last updated November 7, 2022.

83 Amy Gardner, Hannah Knowles, Colby Itkowitz, and Annie Linskey, "Republicans in Key Battleground Races Refuse to Say They Will Accept Results," Washington Post, September 18, 2022.

84 Reid J. Epstein, "Echoing Trump, These Republicans Won't Promise to Accept 2022 Results," New York Times, September 18, 2022.

85 David Leonhardt, "'A Crisis Coming': The Twin Threats to American Democracy," *New York Times*, September 17, 2022.

86 Linda So, "Trump-Inspired Death Threats Are Terrorizing Election Workers," Reuters, June 11, 2021.

87 Geneva Sands, "DHS Updates Terrorism Bulletin in the Wake of Recent Violent Events and Russia-Ukraine Tensions," CNN online, last updated February 7, 2022.

88 Kevin Breuninger, "'You Can't Love Your Country Only When You Win': Biden Urges Americans to Defend the Right to Vote, Condemns Trump Election Lies on Jan. 6 Anniversary," CNBC online, last updated Jan. 6, 2022.

CHAPTER 3: **"A NORMAL TOURIST VISIT"**

1 Sudiksha Kochi, "What to Know About Donald Trump's Jan. 6 Speech—and How It Could Play a Role in Possible Charges," *USA Today*, July 19, 2023.

2 Calvin Woodward, "AP Fact Check: Trump's Call to Action Distorted in Debate," Associated Press, January 13, 2021.

3 Calvin Woodward, "AP Fact Check: Trump's False Claims, Fuel on a Day of Chaos," Associated Press, January 6, 2021.

4 Amanda Macias, "FBI Says There Is 'No Indication' That Antifa Took Part in U.S. Capitol Riot," CNBC online, January 8, 2021.

5 Brandy Zadrozny and Ben Collins, "Trump Loyalists Push Evidence-Free Claims That Antifa Activists Fueled Mob," NBC News online, last updated January 6, 2021.

6 Teo Armus, "Rep. Matt Gaetz and Other GOP Politicians Baselessly Suggest Antifa Is to Blame for Pro-Trump Mob Rioting into Capitol," *Washington Post*, January 7, 2021.

7 Zadrozny and Collins, "Trump Loyalists Push Evidence-Free Claims."

8 Steve Benen, "Trump's Defense Team Creates an Odd Alternate Reality for Senators," MSNBC online, February 12, 2021.

9 Trip Gabriel and Reid J. Epstein, "Assaulting the Truth, Ron Johnson Helps Erode Confidence in Government," *New York Times*, March 21, 2021.

10 Aaron Rupar, "Ron Johnson Uses Senate Hearing on January 6 Insurrection to Push Absurd Conspiracy Theory," Vox, February 23, 2021.

11 Clara Hendrickson and Dave Boucher, "Shirkey Falsely Claims US Capitol Attack Was Staged, Not Carried Out by Trump Supporters," *Detroit Free Press*, February 9, 2021.

12 Summer Concepcion, Zoe Richards, and Matt Shuham, "5 Points on FBI Director Wray's First Congressional Testimony Since Capitol Attack," Talking Points Memo, March 2, 2021.

13 Susan Page and Sarah Elbeshbishi, "Exclusive: Defeated and Impeached, Trump Still Commands the Loyalty of the GOP's Voters," *USA Today*, February 21, 2021.

14 Alan Feuer, Luke Broadwater, Maggie Haberman, Katie Benner, and Michael S. Schmidt, "Jan. 6: The Story So Far," *New York Times*, June 10, 2022.

15 Carl Hulse, "Jan. 6 Panel Hearings: Witness Details Trump's Rage and Meadows's Inaction on Jan. 6," *New York Times*, June 28, 2022.

16 Marshall Cohen, Zachary Cohen, and Alex Rogers, "7 Takeaways from Tuesday's Shocking January 6 Hearing," CNN online, last updated June 29, 2022.

17 Philip Bump, "What Donald Trump Has Said About the Capitol Rioters," *Washington Post*, July 22, 2021.

18 Andrew Restuccia, "Trump in Farewell Address Set to Say: 'We Inaugurate a New Administration and Pray for Its Success,'" *Wall Street Journal*, January 19, 2021.

19 Veronica Stracqualursi, "Trump Lies About Capitol Riot by Claiming His Supporters Were 'Hugging and Kissing' Cops," CNN online, last updated March 26, 2021.

20 Quint Forgey, "Trump: Rioters in Deadly Capitol Insurrection Posed 'Zero Threat,'" *Politico*, March 26, 2021.

21 Molly Ball, "What Mike Fanone Can't Forget," *Time*, August 5, 2021.

22 Chris Cameron, "These Are the People Who Died in Connection with the Capitol Riot," *New York Times*, January 5, 2022.

23 Melissa Quinn, "Trump Claims Crowd at January 6 Rally Before Capitol Assault Was 'Loving,'" CBS News online, July 22, 2021.

24 Bump, "What Donald Trump Has Said About the Capitol Rioters."

25 Cristina Marcos and Rebecca Beitsch, "Five Things to Watch as Jan. 6 Panel Begins Its Work," *The Hill*, July 26, 2021.

26 David Leonhardt and Ian Prasad Philbrick, "Valorizing Jan. 6," *New York Times*, September 17, 2021.

27 Jill Colvin, "AP Fact Check: No, Election Day Wasn't the Real Insurrection," Associated Press, October 21, 2021.

28 Acyn (@Acyn), "Trump: Some of these people are not guilty. Many of these people are not guilty. What they've done to these and in many cases they're patriots. They're soldiers, they're policemen . . . Lindsey Graham doesn't know what the hell he's talking about if he said that," Twitter, February 1, 2022, 10:32 p.m.

29 Brent D. Griffiths, "Trump Says January 6 'Represented the Greatest Movement in the History of Our Country' Ahead of the House Committee's First Public Hearing," Business Insider, June 9, 2022.

30 Mary Papenfuss, "Trump Says He'll Look 'Very Seriously' at Pardoning Jan. 6 Defendants If Reelected," HuffPost, June 17, 2022.

31 Steve Benen, "Trump Is Now Eyeing More Than Just Pardons for Jan. 6 Rioters," MSNBC online, September 2, 2022.

32 Dartunorro Clark, "GOP Sen. Ron Johnson Says He Never Felt Threatened During Jan. 6 Capitol Attack," NBC News online, last updated March 12, 2021.

33 Meena Venkataramanan, "Gosar Calls Jan. 6 US Capitol Attackers 'Peaceful Patriots,' Says Slain Rioter 'Executed,'" *Arizona Republic*, May 12, 2021.

34 Jan Wolfe, "'What Planet' Are They On? Judge Blasts Republicans for Downplaying Attack on U.S. Capitol," Reuters, June 23, 2021.

35 Brittany Shammas, "A GOP Congressman Compared Capitol Rioters to Tourists. Photos Show Him Barricading a Door," *Washington Post*, May 18, 2021.

36 Nia Prater, "Republican Stands By 1/6 'Tourist Visit' Comparison After Searing Testimony by Police," *New York*, July 28, 2021.

37 Lee Moran, "Ex-Defense Secretary Delivers Damning Takedown of GOP Spin on U.S. Capitol Riot," HuffPost, last updated May 15, 2021.

38 Cameron Jenkins, "Kinzinger: GOP Downplaying Capitol Riot Something 'out of North Korea,'" *The Hill*, May 14, 2021.

39 Steve Benen, "Kevin McCarthy Falsely Claims FBI Cleared Trump of Jan. 6 Culpability," MSNBC online, September 7, 2021.

40 Lisa Mascaro, "Marjorie Taylor Greene's Jail Visit Pulls GOP Closer to Jan. 6 Rioters," Associated Press, March 25, 2023.

41 Dana Milbank, "As Jan. 6 Hearings Begin, Republicans Side with the Terrorists," *Washington Post*, July 27, 2021.

42 "Public Supports Wide-Ranging Inquiry, Says White Nationalism Played a Role," Monmouth University Polling Institute, March 17, 2021.

43 Paul LeBlanc, "Here Are the 35 House Republicans Who Voted for the January 6 Commission," CNN online, May 19, 2021.

44 Jamie Gangel and Michael Warren, "McConnell Doubles Down to Pressure Republicans, Asking for 'a Personal Favor' to Block January 6 Commission," CNN online, May 27, 2021.

45 Claudia Grisales, "Nancy Pelosi Rejects 2 GOP Picks for Jan. 6 Inquiry Committee," NPR online, July 21, 2021.

46 Scott Wong, "McCarthy's Jan. 6 Committee Gamble Faces Big Test This Spring," NBC News online, April 10, 2022.

47 Mary Clare Jalonick, Eric Tucker, Farnoush Amiri, Jill Colvin, Michael Balsamo, and Nomaan Merchant, "Jan. 6 Report: Trump 'Lit That Fire' of Capitol Insurrection," Associated Press, December 23, 2022.

48 Isaac Arnsdorf and Maeve Reston, "Trump Claims Violence He Inspired on Jan. 6 Was Pence's Fault," *Washington Post*, March 13, 2023.

49 Kelby Vera, "Donald Trump Finds a Way to Blame Nancy Pelosi for Jan. 6 Insurrection," HuffPost, September 17, 2023.

50 Tori Otten, "Republicans Have a New January 6 Conspiracy Theory: Deep State 'Ghost Buses,'" *The New Republic*, November 15, 2023.

51 Tim Hains, "George Will: 'I'd Like to See January 6 Burned into the American Mind as Firmly as 9/11,'" Real Clear Politics, May 23, 2021.

52 Robert Draper, "Far Right Pushes a Through-the-Looking-Glass Narrative on Jan. 6," *New York Times*, June 23, 2023.

53 Philip Bump, "The Death of Ashli Babbitt Offers the Purest Distillation of Donald Trump's View of Justice," *Washington Post*, July 7, 2021.

54 Steve Benen, "Officer Who Shot Ashli Babbitt Cleared, Contradicting Trump," MSNBC online, August 24, 2021.

55 Luke Broadwater, "Capitol Police Clear Officer Who Shot Rioter, Saying He May Have Saved Lives," *New York Times*, August 23, 2021.

56 Aaron Blake, "The Slow-Building Conservative Effort to Turn Ashli Babbitt into a Martyr," *Washington Post*, June 18, 2021.

57 Josh Marshall, "Trump Demanding Release of Jan 6 Insurrectionists," Talking Points Memo, July 6, 2021.

58 Kelsey Vlamis, "Trump Called Ashli Babbitt an 'Innocent, Wonderful, Incredible Woman' and Suggested Without Evidence That a Democratic Official Was Connected to Her Death," Business Insider, July 11, 2021.

59 Rebecca Falconer, "Trump Calls Officer Who Fatally Shot Rioter Ashli Babbitt a 'Murderer,'" Axios, August 11, 2021.

60 Ursula Perano, "Trump Calls Capitol Police Officer Who Shot Ashli Babbitt a 'Thug,'" Daily Beast, last updated May 10, 2023.

61 Charna Flam, "January 6 Prison Choir's 'Justice for All' Single, Featuring Donald Trump, Reaches No. 1 on iTunes," *Variety*, March 11, 2023.

62 Steve Benen, "Unrepentant, Trump Participates in Fundraiser for Jan. 6 Defendants," MSNBC online, August 25, 2023.

63 Jake Traylor, "Trump Calls People Charged and Convicted for Jan. 6 Riots 'Hostages,'" NBC News online, November 3, 2023.

64 Amy B Wang and Isaac Arnsdorf, "Trump Claims He Peacefully Surrendered Power, Ignoring Jan. 6 Attack," *Washington Post*, December 22, 2023.

65 Garrett Ross, "Playbook PM: GOP Conference Rages Against Border Deal," *Politico*, January 30, 2024.

66 Jordain Carney and Kyle Cheney, "House GOP Flirts with Jan. 6 Extremism," *Politico*, June 18, 2023.

67 Justin Papp, "Loudermilk's First Move on Jan. 6 Is to Clear Himself," *Roll Call*, March 29, 2023.

68 Aaron Blake, "Republican Takes Jan. 6 and Justice Dept. Claims to New Places," *Washington Post*, September 20, 2023.

69 Nikki McCann Ramirez, "MTG Wants to Impeach D.C. DA for Not Letting Jan. 6 Rioters Skate," *Rolling Stone*, May 16, 2023.

70 Mike Allen, "Exclusive: McCarthy Gives Tucker Carlson Access to Trove of Jan. 6 Riot Tape," Axios, February 20, 2023.

71 Annie Grayer, Jamie Gangel, Alayna Treene, and Hannah Rabinowitz, "McCarthy Gives Tucker Carlson Access to January 6 Capitol Security Footage, Sources Say," CNN online, last updated February 21, 2023.

72 Steve Benen, "Tucker Carlson Pushes the Bogus Jan. 6 Story He Wanted to Tell," MSNBC online, March 7, 2023.

73 Sahil Kapur, "Tucker Carlson, with Video Provided by Speaker McCarthy, Falsely Depicts Jan. 6 Riot as a Peaceful Gathering," NBC News online, last updated March 7, 2023.

74 Arthur Delaney, "Tucker Carlson Cherry-Picks Jan. 6 Footage to Deny There Was Any Insurrection," HuffPost, March 7, 2023.

75 Aila Slisco, "Trump Demands Release of Jan. 6 Prisoners After Tucker Carlson's 'Scoop,'" Newsweek, March 7, 2023.

76 Donald J. Trump (@realDonaldTrump), "Great courage shown by Speaker of the House Kevin McCarthy in releasing the surveillance footage to Tucker Carlson so that our Country, and indeed the World, can see what really went on during the January 6th events. A whole new, and completely opposite, picture has now been indelibly painted. The Unselect Committee LIED, and should be prosecuted for their actions. Nancy & Mitch were a disaster on Security. Thank you Kevin and Tucker. FREE AT LAST!!!" Truth Social, March 6, 2023, 9:25 p.m.

77 Donald J. Trump (@realDonaldTrump), " LET THE JANUARY 6 PRISONERS GO. THEY WERE CONVICTED, OR ARE AWAITING TRIAL, BASED ON A GIANT LIE, A RADICAL LEFT CON JOB. THANK YOU TO TUCKER CARLSON AND SPEAKER OF THE HOUSE KEVIN McCARTHY FOR WHAT YOU BOTH HAVE DONE. NEW VIDEO FOOTAGE IS IRREFUTABLE!!!" Truth Social, March 7, 2023, 7:28 a.m.

78 Katherine Faulders, Rachel Scott, and Luke Barr, "Capitol Police Chief Slams Carlson's Comments About Jan. 6 Video as 'Offensive And Misleading' in Internal Memo," ABC News, March 7, 2023.

79 Andrew Solander, "GOP Lawmakers Revisit Trump Impeachments," Axios, June 22, 2023.

80 Page and Elbeshbishi, "Exclusive: Defeated and Impeached."

81 James Oliphant and Chris Kahn, "Half of Republicans Believe False Accounts of Deadly U.S. Capitol Riot—Reuters/Ipsos Poll," Reuters, April 5, 2021.

82 "78% Of Republicans Want to See Trump Run for President in 2024, Quinnipiac University National Poll Finds; Americans Now Split on Border Wall as Opposition Softens," Quinnipiac University, October 19, 2021.

83 Ed Kilgore, "Republicans Exonerate Trump by Whitewashing January 6," *New York*, July 8, 2022.

84 "National: Faith in American System Drops," Monmouth University Polling Institute, July 7, 2022.

85 Ronald Brownstein, "The Threat to Democracy Is Coming from Inside the U.S. House," *The Atlantic*, October 18, 2023.

86 Tom Jackman, Scott Clement, Emily Guskin, and Spencer S. Hsu, "A Quarter of Americans Believe FBI Instigated Jan. 6, Post-UMD Poll Finds," *Washington Post*, January 4, 2024.

87 Brownstein, "The Threat to Democracy Is Coming from Inside."

88 Ryan J. Reilly and Daniel Barnes, "Jan. 6 Rioter Who Dragged Michael Fanone into Crowd Sentenced to 7.5 Years in Prison," NBC News online, October 27, 2022.

89 Ryan J. Reilly, "Reagan-Appointed Judge Warns GOP's 'Preposterous' Claims about Jan. 6 Could Pose Threat," NBC News, January 25, 2024.

CHAPTER 4: **"A PERFECT PHONE CALL"**

1 "Trump Tries to Force Ukraine to Meddle in the 2020 Election," *Washington Post*, editorial, September 5, 2019.

2 Caitlin Emma and Connor O'Brien, "Trump Holds Up Ukraine Military Aid Meant to Confront Russia," *Politico*, last updated August 29, 2019.

3 Justin Doom and Kelly Terez, "Trump Says 'I Think I'd Take' Help If Foreigners Offered Dirt on Political Opponents," ABC News online, June 13, 2019.

4 Karoun Demirjian, Josh Dawsey, Ellen Nakashima, and Carol D. Leonnig, "Trump Ordered Hold on Military Aid Days Before Calling Ukrainian President, Officials Say," *Washington Post*, September 23, 2019.

5 Philip Bump, "Why Trump Releasing the Transcript of His Call with Ukraine's President Isn't Enough," *Washington Post*, September 24, 2019.

6 Josh Wingrove and Jennifer Jacobs, "Trump Suggests He Discussed Biden with Ukraine's Zelenskiy," Bloomberg News, September 22, 2019.

7 Donald Trump (@RealDonaldTrump), "Will the Democrats apologize after seeing what was said on the call with the Ukrainian President? They should, a perfect call—got them by surprise!" Twitter, September 25, 2019, 9:17 a.m.

8 "Read the Trump-Ukraine Phone Call Readout," *Politico*, September 25, 2019.

9   Charlie Savage and Adam Goldman, "The Trump-Zelensky Phone Call: Key Takeaways from Two New Documents," *New York Times*, September 26, 2019.

10 "Transcript: *Meet the Press*—September 22, 2019," NBC News online, last modified September 22, 2019.

11 Philip Bump, "Trump's News Conference with Ukraine's President, Annotated," *Washington Post*, September 25, 2019.

12 Peter Baker and Eileen Sullivan, "Trump Publicly Urges China to Investigate the Bidens," *New York Times*, October 3, 2019.

13 Steve Benen, "As Scandal Intensifies, Testimony Collapses Pillar of Trump Defense," MSNBC online, last updated October 23, 2019.

14 Melanie Zanona, Burgess Everett, and Marianne LeVine, "'No Quid Pro Quo': Trump's Republican Defenders Dig In," *Politico*, September 25, 2019.

15 David A. Graham, "'Get Over It': The Administration Has a Single Answer for Every Question About Its Policies and Behavior," *The Atlantic*, October 18, 2019.

16 Karoun Demirjian and John Hudson, "After Saying Trump Held Back Aid to Pressure Ukraine, Mulvaney Tries to Walk Back Comments," *Washington Post*, October 17, 2019.

17 Allan Smith, "Mulvaney Walks Back His Remarks That Trump Held Up Ukraine Aid for Political Reasons," NBC News online, last updated October 17, 2019.

18 Aaron Blake, "5 Takeaways from William Taylor's Huge Opening Statement," *Washington Post*, October 22, 2019.

19 Franco Ordoñez, "Top Ukraine Expert Reported Concerns About Trump's July Call with Ukraine President," NPR online, October 28, 2019.

20 Josh Lederman and Adam Edelman, "Sondland Changes Testimony, Acknowledges Delivering Quid Pro Quo Message to Ukraine," NBC News online, last updated November 6, 2019.

21 Matt Cohen, "'He's Gonna Do It.' David Holmes Describes Overhearing Trump-Sondland Call," *Mother Jones*, November 21, 2019.

22 Alex Ward, "One of the Republicans' Witnesses Confirmed a Quid Pro Quo on TV," Vox, November 19, 2019.

23 Josh Dawsey, Carol D. Leonnig, and Tom Hamburger, "White House Review Turns Up Emails Showing Extensive Effort to Justify Trump's Decision to Block Ukraine Military Aid," *Washington Post*, November 24, 2019.

24 Maggie Haberman and Annie Karni, "Mulvaney Asked About Legal Justification for Withholding Ukraine Aid," *New York Times*, November 24, 2019.

25 Julie Pace, "Lots of Impeachment Evidence but One Thing Missing," Associated Press, November 21, 2019.

26 Eugene Robinson, "Imagine Defending Trump After This Week's Hearings. Oh, Wait . . . ," *Washington Post*, November 21, 2019.

27   Kyle Cheney and Andrew Desiderio, "Impeachment Surprises Boost Dems, but Republican Resistance Holds," *Politico*, November 21, 2019.

28   MSNBC's Deadline White House (@DeadlineWH), "'I think Donald Trump makes his mental fitness a part of the issue every single day . . . You read that letter that he sent today to the House and it's just six pages of pure crazy, weapons-grade nuts . . . '—@TheRickWilson w/ @NicolleDWallace," Twitter, December 17, 2019, 6:22 p.m.

29   Kevin M. Kruse (@KevinMKruse), "It *is* a historic document and it will be cited by scholars, but only with a lengthy preface that assures readers it was not, in fact, a crayon-scribbled manifesto discovered in the shack of a lunatic," Twitter, December 18, 2019, 7:51 a.m.

30   Matt Zapotosky, "More Than 500 Law Professors Say Trump Committed 'Impeachable Conduct,'" *Washington Post*, December 6, 2019.

31   Felicia Sonmez, "More Than 700 Scholars Pen Letter Urging House to Impeach Trump," *Washington Post*, December 16, 2019.

32   Michael Macagnone and Patrick Kelley, "Most Republicans on Impeachment Committees Aren't Showing Up, Transcripts Reveal," *Roll Call*, November 5, 2019.

33   Steve Benen, "Lindsey Graham Goes from Moving the Goalposts to Eliminating Them," MSNBC online, last updated November 6, 2019.

34   Nicholas Fandos and Michael D. Shear, "Trump Impeached for Abuse of Power and Obstruction of Congress," *New York Times*, December 18, 2019.

35   Lachlan Markay, "Government Accountability Office Finds That Trump White House Illegally Held Up Ukraine Aid," Daily Beast, last updated January 16, 2020.

36   Eric Lipton, Maggie Haberman, and Mark Mazzetti, "Behind the Ukraine Aid Freeze: 84 Days of Conflict and Confusion," *New York Times*, December 29, 2019.

37   Daniel Dale, "Fact Check: 65 Ways Trump Has Been Dishonest About Ukraine and Impeachment," CNN online, January 20, 2020.

38   Toluse Olorunnipa and Philip Rucker, "Trump Makes Falsehoods Central to Impeachment Defense as Incriminating Evidence Mounts," *Washington Post*, November 6, 2019.

39   Philip Bump, "What Trump Allies and Republicans Said About Quid Pro Quo Before the Bolton News," *Washington Post*, January 28, 2020.

40   Mariah Timms, Duane W. Gang, and Joel Ebert, "Sen. Lamar Alexander Defends Witness Vote, Says President's Actions Inappropriate but Don't Warrant Removal," *The Tennessean*, January 31, 2020.

41   Steve Benen, "Multiple Republicans Agree: Trump's Guilty, but It Doesn't Matter," MSNBC online, last updated February 3, 2020.

42 "By a Narrow Margin, Americans Say Senate Trial Should Result in Trump's Removal," Pew Research Center, January 22, 2020.

43 Dana Milbank, "'S.O.S.! PLEASE HELP ME!' The World's Greatest Deliberative Body Falls to Pettifoggery." *Washington Post*, January 22, 2020.

44 Laurie Roberts, "Rep. Debbie Lesko Dives Down the Rabbit Hole to Defend Donald Trump in Impeachment," *Arizona Republic*, December 16, 2019.

45 Steve Benen, "Overcoming the Challenge of Up-Is-Down, Day-Is-Night Politics," MSNBC online, last updated January 23, 2020.

46 Acyn (@acyn), "DeSantis: They opened an impeachment on trump based on a phone call to Ukraine. There's way more evidence for this one," Twitter, September 17, 2023, 11:21 a.m.

47 Ken Buck, "My Fellow Republicans: One Disgraceful Impeachment Doesn't Deserve Another," *Washington Post*, September 15, 2023.

48 Philip Bump, "Does New House Speaker Really Think Biden Impeachment Push Is Apolitical?" *Washington Post*, November 2, 2023.

49 Sheryl Gay Stolberg, "Pelosi Says Democrats Have 'Pulled Back a Veil' on Trump's 'Unacceptable' Behavior," *New York Times*, February 3, 2020.

50 Mairead McArdle, "Trump Says Congress Should Expunge Impeachment from Record," *National Review*, February 7, 2020.

51 Oliver Willis, "GOP Congressman: We'll 'Expunge' Trump Impeachment If We Take Back the House," *American Independent*, February 24, 2020.

52 Tyler Olson, "Mullin Introducing Resolution to Expunge First Trump Impeachment: 'Perfect Phone Call,'" Fox News online, March 29, 2022.

53 John Wagner, "McCarthy Says He's Willing to Look at Expunging a Trump Impeachment," *Washington Post*, January 12, 2023.

54 Mica Soellner, "House GOP Weighs Expunging Donald Trump Impeachments," *Washington Times*, January 12, 2023.

55 Andrew Solender, "GOP Lawmakers Revisit Trump Impeachments," Axios, June 22, 2023.

56 Jacqueline Alemany and Leigh Ann Caldwell, "McCarthy Privately Recounts Terse Phone Call with Trump After Ouster," *Washington Post*, November 30, 2023.

57 Acyn (@acyn), "Mace: I wasn't in congress during the first impeachment, but we know that the basis for that impeachment was based on a bed of lies. The second one, there was a lack of due process, lack of investigation in the House side," Twitter, June 23, 2023, 11:47 p.m.

58 Courtney Subramanian, "Explainer: Biden, Allies Pushed Out Ukrainian Prosecutor Because He Didn't Pursue Corruption Cases," *USA Today*, October 3, 2019.

59 Domenico Montanaro, "Russia's Invasion Puts a New Light on Trump's Ukraine Pressure Campaign," NPR online, March 8, 2022.

60 Grace Segers, "Susan Collins Will Vote to Acquit Trump, Saying He's 'Learned'
    from Impeachment," CBS News online, last updated February 4, 2020.

61 Steve Benen, "Despite Impeachment, Trump Again Wants to Tie Strings to
    Ukraine Aid," MSNBC online, July 31, 2023.

CHAPTER 5: "I DID FINISH THE WALL"

1   Michael Mitsanas, "Chris Christie, Jeered for Criticizing Trump, Tells
    Crowd: 'You Can Boo All You Want,'" NBC News online, last modified
    June 23, 2023.

2   Ken Meyer, "Chris Christie Shuts Down Fox News Anchor's Gushing About
    Trump's Immigration Policies: 'Mexico Hasn't Given Us One Peso' for the
    Wall," Mediaite, June 14, 2023.

3   Donald J. Trump (@RealDonaldTrump), "Reported that Sloppy Chris Chris-
    tie said I only built 50 Miles of Wall on the Southern Border. Wrong! I built
    almost 500 Miles of Wall, including the fact that some very dilapidated ar-
    eas had to be completely demolished with new Wall then built. He knows
    this but keeps repeating the lies. That is why he left New Jersey with a 9%
    Approval Rating, the lowest on record, and is currently polling at around
    2% in the Republican Primary—with nobody showing up at his 'events.'
    Loser!" Truth Social, August 10, 2023, 9:44 p.m.

4   Linda Qiu, "Trump Revives Election Lies and False Boasts in CNN Town
    Hall," New York Times, May 10, 2023.

5   Joshua Green, Devil's Bargain: Steve Bannon, Donald Trump, and the Storming
    of the Presidency (New York: Penguin Press, 2017).

6   Julie Hirschfeld Davis and Peter Baker, "How the Border Wall Is Boxing
    Trump In," New York Times, January 5, 2019.

7   "Editorial: A Chance to Reset the Republican Race," New York Times, Janu-
    ary 30, 2016.

8   Steve Benen, The Impostors: How Republicans Quit Governing and Seized
    American Politics (New York: HarperCollins, 2020).

9   Bob Woodward and Robert Costa, "Trump Reveals How He Would Force
    Mexico to Pay for Border Wall," Washington Post, April 5, 2016.

10 Jessica Estepa, "President Trump, Mexico Trade Barbs over Who's Going to
    Pay for the Wall," USA Today, August 28, 2017.

11 Matt Shuham, "Fox News: DHS Secretary Says Parts of Border Wall Will Be
    'See Through,'" Talking Points Memo, February 2, 2017.

12 "The Latest: Feds Extend Deadline for First Border Wall Bids," Associated
    Press online, last modified March 29, 2017.

13 Nick Gass, "Rick Perry: Trump's Mexico Wall Will Be a 'Digital Wall,'" Politico,
    July 11, 2016.

14   Graham Vyse, "American Taxpayers Are Going to Pay for Donald Trump's Border Wall," *The New Republic*, January 6, 2017.

15   Louis Nelson, "Trump Promises His Mexico Wall Is 'Way Ahead of Schedule,'" *Politico*, February 24, 2017.

16   Steve Benen, "Trump's Vision of a 'Great Wall' Starts to Look Like a Mirage," MSNBC online, March 3, 2017.

17   Mike DeBonis, Ed O'Keefe, and Erica Werner, "Here's What Congress Is Stuffing into Its $1.3 Trillion Spending Bill," *Washington Post*, March 22, 2018.

18   Jen Kirby, "Here Are 6 of the Most Bizarre Things Trump Said in His Infrastructure Speech," Vox, last modified March 29, 2018.

19   Salvador Hernandez, "Trump Tweeted Pictures Claiming 'the Start' of His Border Wall, but It Was Actually an Old Project," BuzzFeed, last modified March 28, 2018.

20   Dan Solomon, "Where Is San Antonio in Relation to the Border? An Investigation That Is Apparently Necessary," *Texas Monthly*, January 25, 2019.

21   Reis Thebault, "Trump and Democrats Are in Parallel Universes When It Comes to the Border," *Washington Post*, January 17, 2019.

22   Gina Martinez, "President Trump Went to a Border Town to Prove They Need a Wall. Residents Say Otherwise," *Time*, January 10, 2019.

23   Lauren Egan, "Trump Visits Border Wall Construction, Calls Technology 'Virtually Impenetrable,'" NBC News online, September 18, 2019.

24   Andy Rose and Paul LeBlanc, "Portion of US Border Wall in California Falls Over in High Winds and Lands on Mexican Side," CNN, January 29, 2020.

25   Rose and LeBlanc, "Portion of US Border Wall in California Falls Over."

26   Steve Benen, "'Impenetrable' Border Wall Damaged by Monsoon Rains in Arizona," MSNBC online, August 24, 2021.

27   Nick Miroff, "Smugglers Are Sawing Through New Sections of Trump's Border Wall," *Washington Post*, November 2, 2019.

28   Nick Miroff, "Trump's Border Wall Has Been Breached More Than 3,000 Times by Smugglers, CBP Records Show," *Washington Post*, March 2, 2022.

29   Kate Rabinowitz and Aaron Steckelberg, "Trump's Changing Vision of the Wall," *Washington Post*, January 11, 2019.

30   Rabinowitz and Steckelberg, "Trump's Changing Vision of the Wall."

31   Gus Bova, "Federal Judge Dismisses Butterfly Refuge's Lawsuit over Wall Construction," *Texas Observer*, February 11, 2019.

32   Aaron Rupar (@atrupar), "Trump now claims he actually finished the border wall," Twitter, July 22, 2022, 11:10 p.m.

33   Aaron Rupar (@atrupar), "Big news, folks—Trump says he actually completed the wall after all. Our border problems are solved," Twitter, August 6, 2022, 1:35 a.m.

34 Aaron Rupar (@atrupar), "In the same statement Trump claims he both built the wall and would've had the wall built in three more weeks," Twitter, September 20, 2022, 9:12 a.m.

35 Aaron Rupar (@atrupar), "'The wall was completed'—Donald Trump," Twitter, September 21, 2022, 9:15 p.m.

36 Donald J. Trump (@RealDonaldTrump), "I built 561 Miles of Border Wall between the United States and Mexico, as per the highest specifications of Brandon Judd and the U.S. Border Patrol, with the great Tom Homan consulting. This was more than the 400 Miles that I said I was going to build, and despite the false promises of the Broken Old Crow, Mitch McConnell, and RINO Paul RINO. Crazy Nancy & Cryin' Chuck Schumer (a friend of Judge Engoron?) fought me all the way. What a group? But I got the Wall built anyway, and more was coming, until Crooked Joe, instead of installing it, sold it for pennies on the dollar (Did he know the buyer?). Now, after 15,000,000 people, many from prisons and mental institutions, have invaded our Country, this corrupt & incompetent president wants to put up a small, below spec, 20 mile Wall. Has he apologized to me yet?" Truth Social, October 7, 2023, 11:52 a.m.

37 Donald J. Trump (@RealDonaldTrump), "With Mexico being one of the highest crime Nations in the world, we must have THE WALL. Mexico will pay for it through reimbursement/other," Twitter, August 27, 2017, 9:44 a.m.

38 Aaron Blake, "Sorry, Trump Supporters: The White House Clearly Isn't Going to Make Mexico Pay for That Wall," *Washington Post*, August 24, 2017.

39 Donald J. Trump (@RealDonaldTrump), "I often stated, 'One way or the other, Mexico is going to pay for the Wall.' This has never changed. Our new deal with Mexico (and Canada), the USMCA, is so much better than the old, very costly & anti-USA NAFTA deal, that just by the money we save, MEXICO IS PAYING FOR THE WALL!" Twitter, December 13, 2018, 7:38 a.m.

40 Donald J. Trump (@RealDonaldTrump), "Mexico is paying for the Wall through the new USMCA Trade Deal. Much of the Wall has already been fully renovated or built. We have done a lot of work. $5.6 Billion Dollars that House has approved is very little in comparison to the benefits of National Security. Quick payback!" Twitter, January 2, 2019, 8:35 a.m.

41 Linda Qiu, "Trump's Baseless Claim That Mexico Will Pay for the Wall Through the New Nafta," *New York Times*, December 13, 2018.

42 Steve Benen, "Despite Reality, Trump Insists Mexico Is 'Paying for the Wall,'" MSNBC online, March 3, 2020.

43 Hope Yen and Calvin Woodward, "AP Fact Check: Trump's Wall Claim Is Beyond 'Redemption,'" Associated Press, February 15, 2020.

44 Emily Stewart, "Let's Look Back at Trump's Actual Plan for Making Mexico Pay for the Wall," Vox, January 10, 2019.

45 Steve Benen, "Defying Reality, Trump Insists Mexico 'Is Paying for the Wall,'" MSNBC online, September 9, 2020.

46   Steve Benen, "Trump Struggles to Defend Lie About Mexico 'Paying for the Wall,'" MSNBC online, October 22, 2020.

47   Nikki McCann Ramirez, "Trump Tries for Sympathy During Fox Town Hall, Says Probe 'Bothers Me,'" *Rolling Stone*, July 18, 2023.

48   Burgess Everett, "Rick Scott Pushes Own GOP Agenda as McConnell Holds Off," *Politico*, February 22, 2022.

49   Sahil Kapur, "5 Takeaways from Biden's State of the Union Speech," NBC News online, March 1, 2022.

50   Alex Thompson and Stef W. Kight, "GOP Presidential Field Embraces Trump's Border Wall," Axios, June 26, 2023.

51   Acyn (@Acyn), "DeSantis: We will build the wall. We will actually have Mexico pay for it," Twitter, January 10, 2024, 9:26 p.m.

52   Quinnipiac University Polling, "85% of Voters Concerned Israel-Hamas War Will Escalate into a Wider War in the Middle East, Quinnipiac University National Poll Finds; Approval for Building Border Wall with Mexico Reaches Record High," press release, October 17, 2023.

CHAPTER 6: **"NUCLEAR-GRADE BANANAS"**

1   Robert Costa and Philip Rucker, "Woodward Book: Trump Says He Knew Coronavirus Was 'Deadly' and Worse Than the Flu While Intentionally Misleading Americans," *Washington Post*, September 9, 2020.

2   Costa and Rucker, "Woodward Book."

3   Kevin Freking and Zeke Miller, "Book: Trump Said of Virus, 'I Wanted to Always Play It Down,'" Associated Press, September 9, 2020.

4   Daniel Dale, Marshall Cohen, Tara Subramaniam, and Holmes Lybrand, "Fact-Checking Trump's Attempt to Erase His Previous Coronavirus Response," CNN online, last updated April 1, 2020.

5   Tommy Bear, "All the Times Trump Compared Covid-19 to the Flu, Even After He Knew Covid-19 Was Far More Deadly," *Forbes*, September 10, 2020.

6   Alana Wise, "Trump Admits Playing Down Coronavirus's Severity, According to New Woodward Book," NPR online, September 9, 2020.

7   Conor Friedersdorf, "Coronavirus: Is Trump Lying or Clueless?" *The Atlantic*, May 19, 2020.

8   Ashley Parker, Yasmeen Abutaleb, and Lena H. Sun, "Squandered Time: How the Trump Administration Lost Control of the Coronavirus Crisis," *Washington Post*, March 7, 2020.

9   Kevin Breuninger, "Media's Coronavirus Stories Trying to Hurt Trump, Mick Mulvaney Says as He Urges Public to Turn Off TV," CNBC online, last updated February 28 2020.

10   Steve Benen, "Team Trump Makes 'Political Calculation,' Puts Burdens on Governors," MSNBC online, April 13, 2020.

11 Steve Benen, "Just How Many Virus Task Forces Does the White House Have?" MSNBC online, April 16, 2020.

12 Jonathan Martin and Maggie Haberman, "Trump Keeps Talking. Some Republicans Don't Like What They're Hearing," *New York Times*, April 9, 2020.

13 Tessa Berenson, "'He's Walking the Tightrope.' How Donald Trump Is Getting Out His Message on Coronavirus," *Time*, March 30, 2020.

14 Steve Benen, "On Multiple Fronts, Trump Clashes with Public-Health Experts," MSNBC online, April 6, 2020.

15 Orion Rummler, "Infectious-Disease Expert: Scott Atlas' Herd Immunity Claims Are 'Pseudoscience,'" Axios, October 18, 2020.

16 Pien Huang, "Trump And WHO: How Much Does the U.S. Give? What's the Impact of a Halt in Funding?" NPR online, April 15, 2020.

17 Cristina Cabrera, "Trump Boosts False Conspiracy Theory That Doctors and CDC Are 'Lying' About COVID," Talking Points Memo, July 13, 2020.

18 Adam Edelman and Dareh Gregorian, "Trump Contradicts CDC Director on Covid-19 Vaccines After Biden Slams President's Promises," NBC News online, last updated September 16, 2020.

19 Rebecca Shabad, "Trump White House Made 'Deliberate Efforts' to Undermine Covid Response, Report Says," NBC News online, December 17, 2021.

20 Noah Weiland, "'Like a Hand Grasping': Trump Appointees Describe the Crushing of the C.D.C.," *New York Times*, December 16, 2020.

21 Matthew Perrone and Kevin Freking, "Panel: Trump Staffers Pushed Unproven COVID Treatment at FDA," Associated Press, August 24, 2022.

22 Susan B. Glasser, "Has Trump Reached the Lying-to-Himself-and-Believing-It Stage of the Coronavirus Pandemic?" *The New Yorker*, May 7, 2020.

23 Libby Cathey, "Trump Downplays Calls for Greater Testing, Suggesting They're Motivated by Politics," ABC News online, May 11, 2020.

24 Charles M. Blow, "Can We Call Trump a Killer?" *New York Times*, June 24, 2020.

25 John Fritze and Adrianna Rodriguez, "Trump Describes Coronavirus Testing as 'Overrated' and Calls for Less If Virus Reemerges," *USA Today*, June 18, 2020.

26 Chris Cillizza, "You Won't Believe What Donald Trump Just Said About Coronavirus Testing," CNN online, last updated July 14, 2020.

27 Erica Werner and Jeff Stein, "Trump Administration Pushing to Block New Money for Testing, Tracing and CDC in Upcoming Coronavirus Relief Bill," *Washington Post*, July 18, 2020.

28 Jonathan Swan, "Watch the Full 'Axios on HBO' Interview with President Trump," Axios, last updated August 4, 2020.

29 "CDC Museum COVID-19 Timeline," Centers for Disease Control and Prevention, last updated July 8, 2022.

30 Benjamin Mueller and Eleanor Lutz, "U.S. Has Far Higher Covid Death Rate Than Other Wealthy Countries," *New York Times*, February 1, 2022.

31 Cameron Peters, "Watch: Trump's Oval Office Address on the Coronavirus," Vox, March 11, 2020.

32 Philip Bump, "Since Imploring His Opponents Not to Politicize Coronavirus, Trump Has Repeatedly Politicized It," *Washington Post*, March 13, 2020.

33 Eric Kleefeld, "Trump Repeats Lie from Sean Hannity About Obama and the H1N1 Flu," Media Matters, March 12, 2020.

34 Aaron Blake, "Trump Calls Obama's Response to Swine Flu 'a Disaster.' Here's What Really Happened," *Washington Post*, March 13, 2020.

35 Steve Benen, "On H1N1, Trump Keeps Pushing a Fight He Simply Cannot Win," MSNBC online, June 18, 2020.

36 Donald Trump (@realDonaldTrump), "Biden got failing grades and polls on his clueless handling of the Swine Flu H1N1. It was a total disaster, they had no idea what they were doing. Among the worst ever!" Twitter, June 18, 2020, 8:43 a.m.

37 Donald J. Trump (@realDonaldTrump), "Why didn't the I.G., who spent 8 years with the Obama Administration (Did she Report on the failed H1N1 Swine Flu debacle where 17,000 people died?), want to talk to the Admirals, Generals, V.P. & others in charge, before doing her report. Another Fake Dossier!" Twitter, April 7, 2020, 11:22 a.m.

38 David Knowles, "Trump, for Some Reason, Compares Coronavirus Death Toll (over 98,000) to That of Swine Flu (Under 20,000)," Yahoo News, May 26, 2020.

39 Blake, "Trump Calls Obama's Response to Swine Flu 'a Disaster.'"

40 Nicholas Kristof (@NickKristof), "The Obama administration's handling of H1N1 was a model. Prompt response, quick development of a vaccine and then messaging for people to get vaccinated. But Rush Limbaugh and Fox News urged people not to get vaccinated, as did Donald Trump himself," Twitter, April 6, 2020, 7:34 p.m.

41 Philip Bump, "Trump May Want to Be a Bit More Judicious About Referring to Pandemics as 'Debacles,'" *Washington Post*, April 10, 2020.

42 "CDC Museum COVID-19 Timeline," Centers for Disease Control and Prevention, last updated July 8, 2022.

43 Elizabeth Cohen and John Bonifield, "Trump Falsely Claimed That Obama Administration Slowed Down Diagnostic Testing," CNN online, last updated March 6, 2020.

44 Rebecca Shabad, "'Should Have Kept His Mouth Shut': McConnell Slams Obama for Criticizing Trump Admin," NBC News online, last updated May 12, 2020.

45 Dan Diamond and Nahal Toosi, "Trump Team Failed to Follow NSC's Pandemic Playbook," *Politico*, March 25, 2020.

46 Diamond and Toosi, "Trump Team Failed."

47 Nahal Toosi, Daniel Lippman, and Dan Diamond, "Before Trump's Inauguration, a Warning: 'The Worst Influenza Pandemic Since 1918,'" *Politico*, March 16, 2020.

48 Beth Cameron, "I Ran the White House Pandemic Office. Trump Closed It," *Washington Post*, March 13, 2020.

49 Conor Friedersdorf, "Trump Defended Cuts to Public-Health Agencies, on Video," *The Atlantic*, March 17, 2020.

50 Michael D. Shear, "Trump Extends Social Distancing Guidelines Through End of April," *New York Times*, March 29, 2020.

51 Jill Colvin, Will Weissert, Zeke Miller, and Aamer Madhani, "Surging Coronavirus Colors White House Race in Closing Days," Associated Press, October 25, 2020.

52 Dareh Gregorian and Shannon Pettypiece, "Trump, Biden Tout Polar-Opposite Coronavirus Messages in Midwest Barnstorm," NBC News online, last updated October 30, 2020.

53 Shane Croucher, "Trump Comments About Hospital Mask Thefts Spark Backlash from Doctors," Newsweek, March 30, 2020.

54 Hope Yen and Calvin Woodward, "AP Fact Check: Trump's Baseless Claim of 'Deep State' at FDA," Associated Press, August 24, 2020.

55 Dareh Gregorian, "Fauci Calls White House Attempts to Discredit Him 'Bizarre,'" NBC News, July 15, 2020.

56 Chris Murphy (@ChrisMurphyCT), "Don't let this feel normal. It's nuclear-grade bananas to have White House staff sending reporters opposition research on their own top infectious disease doctor in the middle of a worsening pandemic that has already killed 130,000," Twitter, July 12, 2020, 12:08 p.m.

57 Steve Benen, "The White House Campaign Against Anthony Fauci Takes a Bizarre Turn," MSNBC online, July 15, 2020.

58 Quint Forgey, "'Fauci's a Disaster': Trump Attacks Health Officials in Fiery Campaign Call," *Politico*, last updated October 19, 2020.

59 Libby Cathey, "Timeline: Tracking Trump Alongside Scientific Developments on Hydroxychloroquine," ABC News online, August 8, 2020.

60 Sarah Owermohle and Dan Diamond, "Trump's Push for Risky Malaria Drugs Disrupts Coronavirus Response," *Politico*, March 27, 2020.

61 Jill Colvin and Jonathan Lemire, "Trump Defends His Role, Differs with Health Expert," Associated Press, March 21, 2020.

62 Dartunorro Clark, "Trump Suggests 'Injection' of Disinfectant to Beat Coronavirus and 'Clean' the Lungs," NBC News online, last updated April 24, 2020.

63 Joe Palca, "NIH Panel Recommends Against Drug Combination Promoted by Trump for COVID-19," NPR online, April 21, 2020.

64 "'What Do You Have to Lose?' How Trump Has Promoted Malaria Drug," video, *New York Times*, April 22, 2020.

65 Zeke Miller, Marilynn Marchione, and Jonathan Lemire, "My 'Decision to Make': Trump Defends Criticized Use of Drug," Associated Press, May 19, 2020.

66 Roni Caryn Rabin and Chris Cameron, "Trump Falsely Claims '99 Percent' of Virus Cases Are 'Totally Harmless,'" *New York Times*, July 5, 2020.

67 Aaron Rupar, "'It Affects Virtually Nobody': Trump Erases Coronavirus Victims as US Death Toll Hits 200,000," Vox, September 22, 2020.

68 Donald J. Trump (@realDonaldTrump), "Cases up because we TEST, TEST, TEST. A Fake News Media Conspiracy. Many young people who heal very fast. 99.9%. Corrupt Media conspiracy at all time high. On November 4th., topic will totally change. VOTE!" Twitter, October 26, 2020, 8:46 a.m.

69 Donald J. Trump (@realDonaldTrump), "We have made tremendous progress with the China Virus, but the Fake News refuses to talk about it this close to the Election. COVID, COVID, COVID is being used by them, in total coordination, in order to change our great early election numbers. Should be an election law violation!" Twitter, October 26, 2020, 7:36 a.m.

70 Aaron Blake and JM Rieger, "Timeline: The 201 Times Trump Has Downplayed the Coronavirus Threat," *Washington Post*, November 3, 2020.

71 Matthew J. Belvedere, "Trump Says He Trusts China's Xi on Coronavirus and the US Has It 'Totally Under Control,'" CNBC online, January 22, 2020.

72 Blake and Rieger, "Timeline."

73 Luke O'Neil, "How Trump Changed His Tune on Coronavirus Again and Again . . . and Again," *The Guardian*, March 18, 2020.

74 Sanjana Karanth, "Trump on His Response to Coronavirus: 'I'd Rate It a 10,'" HuffPost, last updated March 16, 2020.

75 Steve Benen, "As US Death Toll Tops 200,000, Trump Moves the Goalposts (Again)," MSNBC online, September 21, 2020.

76 Steve Benen, "The Problem with Trump's Report Card on His Coronavirus Performance," MSNBC online, September 28, 2020.

77 Zoe Richards, "Trump Says 'Not Much' He Would Change in Hypothetical COVID Do-Over," Talking Points Memo, October 21, 2020.

78 Aaron Rupar (@atrupar), "'Thank God for the genius of the Trump administration'—Sen. Tim Scott," Twitter, March 12, 2021, 10:13 a.m.

79 Eliza Relman, "Trump Dismisses COVID-19 Booster Shots as a 'Money-Making Operation' for Pfizer," Business Insider, August 18, 2021.

80 Relman, "Trump Dismisses COVID-19 Booster Shots."

81 Joseph Guzman, "Trump's White House Doctor Calls Omicron a Midterm Elections Trick," *The Hill*, November 29, 2021.

82   Joseph Gerth, "Rand Paul Says Feds Are Trying to Kill Conservatives. His COVID Claims Embarrass All of Us," *Louisville Courier Journal*, January 28, 2022.

83   Matthew Perrone, "FDA Halts Use of Antibody Drugs That Don't Work vs. Omicron," Associated Press, January 24, 2022.

84   Tara Suter, "Rand Paul Says 'Without Question' Fauci Belongs in Jail," *The Hill*, October 6, 2023.

85   Erik Uebelacker, "Ron Johnson Says COVID Was 'Pre-Planned' in Batsh*t Fox News Rant," Daily Beast, August 11, 2023.

86   Bill Glauber, "Republican U.S. Sen. Ron Johnson Suspended for a Week from YouTube After Milwaukee Press Club Event," *Milwaukee Journal Sentinel*, June 12, 2021.

87   Ron Filipkowski (@RonFilipkowski), "New interview of Trump: 'Biden did a lousy job with covid. We handed him over a great situation and a lot of stupid decisions were made,'" Twitter, September 1, 2023, 3:44 p.m.

88   MJ Lee, "Biden Inheriting Nonexistent Coronavirus Vaccine Distribution Plan and Must Start 'from Scratch,' Sources Say," CNN online, last updated January 21, 2021.

89   Jonah Goldberg, "Come On, President Biden. Set Some Loftier COVID Vaccination Goals," *Los Angeles Times*, January 26, 2021.

90   Peter Baker, "For Trump, Coronavirus Proves to Be an Enemy He Can't Tweet Away," *New York Times*, March 8, 2020.

91   Aaron Rupar (@atrupar), "Trump: '"The one thing I have never been credit for is the job we did on covid.' Oh, he got credit for it in November 2020," Twitter, January 22, 2024.

92   "Biden Tops Trump by 10 Points Among Likely Voters, Quinnipiac University National Poll Finds; Nearly 6 in 10 Say the Country Is Worse Off Than It Was in 2016," Quinnipiac University, September 2, 2020.

93   Domenico Montanaro, "Poll: Biden Takes Double-Digit Lead over Trump," NPR online, October 15, 2020.

94   Fadel Allassan, "Poll: 51% of Republicans Trust Trump on Coronavirus More Than the CDC," Axios, September 23, 2020.

95   Martin Pengelly, "Trump Booed After Telling Supporters to Get Covid Vaccine," *The Guardian*, August 22, 2021.

96   Dan Merica, "Trump Met with Boos After Revealing He Received Covid-19 Booster," CNN online, last updated December 21, 2021.

97   Abigail Weinberg, "Trump Will Say Literally Anything—Except 'Vaccines,'" *Mother Jones*, July 10, 2022.

98   Bess Levin, "Donald Trump Demands Americans Picture His Face While COVID Vaccine Enters Their Bodies," *Vanity Fair*, March 11, 2021.

99   Aaron Rupar (@atrupar), "Trump vows to defund any school (including colleges) that have vaccine mandates," Twitter, June 10, 2023, 4:10 p.m.

100 Steven Shepard, "Our New Poll Shows Just How Much GOP Voters Have Diverged from Everyone Else on Vaccines," *Politico*, September 23, 2023.

101 Annie Linskey, Fenit Nirappil, and Ian Duncan, "Ban on Vaccine Mandates in Texas Sharpens Political Battle Lines," *Washington Post*, October 12, 2021.

102 Shepard, "Our New Poll."

CHAPTER 7: **"THE GREATEST ECONOMY IN THE HISTORY OF THE WORLD"**

1   Steve Benen, "Multiple Republicans Agree: Trump's Guilty, But It Doesn't Matter," MSNBC online, last modified February 3, 2020.

2   Barbara Sprunt, "7 GOP Senators Voted to Convict Trump. Only 1 Faces Voters Next Year," NPR, February 15, 2021.

3   "CNN Transcript: CNN's Jake Tapper Speaks with Sen. Pat Toomey on CNN's State of the Union," CNN online, last modified September 26, 2021.

4   Yacob Reyes, "GOP Sen. Barrasso Declines to Criticize Trump for Defending Threats to 'Hang' Pence," Axios, November 14, 2021.

5   Savannah Behrmann, "Sen. Grassley Said Fox News Failed Trump with Second-Term Agenda Question, Isn't Working to Get Him Re-elected," *USA Today*, last modified June 20, 2020.

6   David Barstow, Susanne Craig, and Russ Buettner, "Trump Engaged in Suspect Tax Schemes as He Reaped Riches from His Father," *New York Times*, October 2, 2018.

7   Russ Buettner and Susanne Craig, "Decade in the Red: Trump Tax Figures Show over $1 Billion in Business Losses," *New York Times*, May 8, 2019.

8   Russ Buettner, Susanne Craig, and Mike McIntire, "Long-Concealed Records Show Trump's Chronic Losses and Years of Tax Avoidance," *New York Times*, September 27, 2020.

9   Emma Brown, "Donald Trump Billed His 'University' as a Road to Riches, But Critics Call It a Fraud," *Washington Post*, September 13, 2015.

10 Brown, "Donald Trump Billed His 'University' as a Road to Riches."

11 Doug Stanglin, "Trump Settles Fraud Case Against Trump University for $25M," *USA Today*, November 18, 2016.

12 Evan Horowitz, "Which President Was the Greatest Jobs Creator?" *Boston Globe*, January 11, 2017.

13 Patricia Cohen, "U.S. Economy Grew at 2.6% Rate in Fourth Quarter," *New York Times*, January 26, 2018.

14 John W. Schoen, "Trump Defies Data with 6% GDP Growth Forecast," CNBC online, December 6, 2017.

15 Eric Levitz, "Trump Predicts 9 Percent Growth, Budget Surplus by End of Presidency," *New York*, July 27, 2018.

16 Steve Benen, "Obama Targets an Overlooked Trump Vulnerability: His Jobs Record," MSNBC online, October 28, 2020.

17 Steve Benen, "It'd Be Great If Trump Were Right About the Economy, But He's Not," MSNBC online, last modified January 29, 2018.

18 Catherine Rampell, "Trump Thinks Rising Stock Prices Mean His Presidency Is Awesome. He's Wrong," *Washington Post*, January 8, 2018.

19 Steve Benen, "Trump's Exaggerations on Jobs Are Wrong and Unnecessary," MSNBC online, last modified June 5, 2018.

20 Donald J. Trump (@RealDonaldTrump), "We are breaking all Jobs and Economic Records but, importantly, our Country has TREMENDOUS FUTURE POTENTIAL. We have just begun!" Twitter, September 8, 2018, 10:51 a.m.

21 Senator Lindsey Graham (@LindseyGrahamSC), "If @BarackObama's jobs numbers were anywhere close to what we're talking about with President @realDonaldTrump. . . . . . the media would stop the Earth from rotating to make sure everybody heard about it!" Twitter, November 5, 2018, 10:30 a.m.

22 Philip Bump, "Trump Loves To Celebrate The Economy—Even Though It Improved Faster In Obama's Second Term," *Washington Post*, October 30, 2019.

23 Lesley Stahl, "The 60 Minutes Interview That President Trump Cut Short," CBS News online, October 26, 2020.

24 Hope Yen, Christopher Rugaber, and Calvin Woodward, "AP Fact Check: Trump's Farewell Falsehoods," Associated Press, January 19, 2021.

25 Chris Cillizza, "The 51 Most Outlandish Lines from Donald Trump's Announcement Speech," CNN online, November 16, 2022.

26 "Fox News Transcript: Hannity," *Hannity*, Fox News, October, 26, 2023.

27 Melanie Trottman, "Donald Trump Calls for $10 Hourly Minimum Wage, Breaks from GOP Position," *Wall Street Journal*, July 27, 2016.

28 Jim Zarroli, "Reality Check: What Donald Trump Has Said About Taxes and the Wealthy," NPR, May 13, 2016.

29 Samantha Jacoby, Senior Tax Legal Analyst, Center on Budget and Policy Priorities, congressional testimony, Senate Budget Committee, May 17, 2023.

30 Derek Thompson, "The GOP Tax Cuts Didn't Work," *The Atlantic*, October 31, 2019.

31 "$1.5 Trillion Tax Cut Had No Major Impact on Business Spending," Reuters, January 28, 2019.

32 Allan Sloan and Cezary Podkul, "Donald Trump Built a National Debt So Big (Even Before the Pandemic) That It'll Weigh Down the Economy for Years," ProPublica, January 14, 2021.

33 Emily Stewart, "Corporate Stock Buybacks Are Booming, Thanks to the Republican Tax Cuts," Vox, last modified March 22, 2018.

34 Brian Faler, "Senate Passes Tax Bill, Teeing Up Final House Vote," Politico, last modified December 20, 2017.

35 Steve Benen, "As Midterm Elections Near, Republicans Largely Ignore Their Tax Plan," MSNBC online, last modified September 14, 2018.

36 Catherine Rampell, "The Republican Tax Cut Is a Big, Fat Failure," Washington Post, October 22, 2018.

37 Dana Blanton, "Fox News Poll: Biden-Trump a 5-Point Race in Post-Convention Poll," Fox News online, September 13, 2020.

38 Alexander Burns and Jonathan Martin, "Trump Onslaught Against Biden Falls Short of a Breakthrough," New York Times, September 12, 2020.

39 Mark Murray, "Poll: Abortion, Trump Boost Midterm Prospects for Democrats," NBC News online, September 18, 2022.

40 Steve Benen, "When It Comes to the Economy, How Does Tim Scott Define 'Worse'?" MSNBC online, July 3, 2023.

41 Benen, "When It Comes to the Economy."

42 Acyn (@acyn), "Trump on Jobs Numbers: Now you're given phony numbers because far fewer people are looking for jobs," Twitter, September 8, 2023, 9:49 p.m.

43 Charles Creitz, "Trump Flames Biden's Economy, Attacks on 'MAGA': He 'Wouldn't Know' What It Means," Fox Business online, August 17, 2023.

44 Jeff Stein, "Trump Advisers Plot Aggressive New Tax Cuts for Second White House Term," Washington Post, last modified September 13, 2023.

45 Frank Newport, "U.S. Public Opinion and the 2017 Tax Law," Gallup, April 29, 2019.

46 Joey Garrison and Maureen Groppe, "Inflation Is Weighing Down Americans. Many Trust Trump, More Than Biden, to Fix It," USA Today, last updated September 14, 2023.

EPILOGUE: "AN ARTIFICIAL VERSION OF HISTORY"

1 Patrick Radden Keefe, "How Mark Burnett Resurrected Donald Trump as an Icon of American Success," The New Yorker, December 27, 2018.

2 Patrick Radden Keefe, "How Mark Burnett Resurrected Donald Trump."

3 Nancy Armour, "Trump Is No 'Ally of Peaceful Protesters,' Whether It's NFL Players or Citizens," USA Today, June 2, 2020.

4 "The History and Heritage of the Church of the Presidents," Library of Congress online.

5 Zach Montague, "Holding It Aloft, He Incited a Backlash. What Does the Bible Mean to Trump?" New York Times, June 2, 2020.

6   Katie Rogers, "Protesters Dispersed with Tear Gas So Trump Could Pose at Church," *New York Times*, June 1, 2020.

7   Jonathan Swan, "Trump Goes Full Law-and-Order," Axios, June 2, 2020.

8   Jake Sherman and Anna Palmer, "Washington Can't Fix This," *Politico*, June 2, 2020.

9   Helene Cooper, Eric Schmitt, and Thomas Gibbons-Neff, "Milley, America's Top General, Walks into a Political Battle," *New York Times*, June 5, 2020.

10 Robert Burns, "Military Chief: Wrong to Walk with Trump Past Park Protest," Associated Press, June 11, 2020.

11 Katie Rogers, "Protesters Dispersed with Tear Gas So Trump Could Pose at Church."

12 Ben Gittleson and Jordyn Phelps, "Trump Denies Ordering Protesters Forcibly Removed for Church Photo Op," ABC News online, June 3, 2020.

13 Donald Trump (@realDonaldTrump), "You got it wrong! If the protesters were so peaceful, why did they light the Church on fire the night before? People liked my walk to this historic place of worship! Sen. Susan Collins, Sen. James Lankford, Sen. Ben Sasse. Please read @MZHemingway below," Twitter, June 2, 2020, 10:28 p.m.

14 Ashley Parker and Robert Costa, "Trump and Allies Try to Rewrite History on Handling of Police Brutality Protests," *Washington Post*, June 3, 2020.

15 Parker and Costa, "Trump and Allies Try to Rewrite History."

16 Zoe Richards, "Kellyanne Conway Blasts Bishop Outraged over Trump's Church Photo Op," Talking Points Memo, June 2, 2020.

17 Philip Bump, "Timeline: The Clearing of Lafayette Square," *Washington Post*, June 5, 2020.

18 Richards, "Kellyanne Conway Blasts Bishop."

19 Ken Dilanian, "Police Did Not Clear D.C.'s Lafayette Square of Protesters So Trump Could Hold a Photo Op, New Report Says," NBC News online, June 9, 2021.

20 Aamer Madhani and Zeke Miller, "White House: Trump Church Visit Akin to Churchill WWII Role," Associated Press, June 3, 2020.

21 Morgan Chalfant, "Trump Says Removal of Protesters 'Handled Very Well,'" *The Hill*, June 3, 2020.

22 Steve Benen, "Why the RNC's Post-Election 'Review' Is Tough to Take Seriously," MSNBC online, November 30, 2022.

23 Steve Benen, "In Historical Terms, Biden's First Midterms Were a Clear Success," MSNBC online, December 7, 2022.

24 Donald Trump (@realDonaldTrump), "WE WON! Pelosi is gone, we take Congress and, if we can stop their very obvious CHEATING, will also take the Senate. Big Victory, don't be stupid. Stand on the rooftops and shout it out loud!" Truth Social, November 11, 2022, 7:44 a.m.

25 Josephine Harvey, "GOP Lawmaker Offers Most Ridiculous Take Yet on Not Prosecuting Trump," HuffPost, August 15, 2022.

26 Paul Fanlund, "Some Republicans Turn on Trump; Ron Johnson's Fealty Grows," Capital Times, June 16, 2023.

27 Louis Nelson, "Trump Ratchets Up Call for DOJ to Investigate Hillary Clinton," Politico, November 3, 2017.

28 Michael S. Schmidt and Maggie Haberman, "Trump Wanted to Order Justice Dept. to Prosecute Comey and Clinton," New York Times, November 20, 2018.

29 Steve Benen, "Does Team Trump Realize That Hillary Clinton Isn't Running?" MSNBC online, October 19, 2020.

30 Steve Benen, "Lobbying Barr, Trump Demands Prosecutions of His Political Foes," MSNBC online, October 8, 2020.

31 Charles Creitz, "DeSantis: Trump Never 'Drained the Swamp,' but I Did in Florida," Fox News online, August 16, 2023.

32 Max Tani, "Exclusive: Trump Defends Family Separation, Warns 'Weaponized' Government Could Target His Opponents, in Univision Sitdown," Semafor, November 9, 2023.

33 Peter Baker, "Trump Claims He's a Victim of Tactics He Once Deployed," New York Times, August 10, 2022.

34 Aaron Blake, "Geoffrey Berman's Big Claims About Trump's Justice Department," Washington Post, September 8, 2022.

35 Aaron Blake, "Trump's Ever-Present—and Still Growing—Exploitation of the Justice Department," Washington Post, June 11, 2021.

36 Doyle McManus, "Trump's Demonization of Biden is Not Normal," Los Angeles Times, October 14, 2020.

37 Donald Trump (@realDonaldTrump), "Obama, Biden, Crooked Hillary and many others got caught in a Treasonous Act of Spying and Government Overthrow, a Criminal Act. How is Biden now allowed to run for President?" Twitter, October 7, 2020, 8:15 p.m.

38 Kyle Cheney, "'Where Are All of the Arrests?': Trump Demands Barr Lock Up His Foes," Politico, October 7, 2020.

39 Aaron Rupar (@atrupar), "'Unless Bill Barr indicts these people for crimes—the greatest political crime in history of our country—then we'll get little satisfaction . . . and that includes Obama and that includes Biden'—Trump calls for Obama and Biden to be charged with crimes," Twitter, October 8, 2020, 8:23 a.m.

40 Michael S. Schmidt, "Trump Wanted I.R.S. Investigations of Foes, Top Aide Says," New York Times, November 13, 2022.

41 Jennifer Agiesta and Ariel Edwards-Levy, "CNN Poll: GOP Voters' Broad Support for Trump Holds, with Less Than Half Seriously Worried Criminal Charges Will Harm His 2024 Chances," CNN online, September 5, 2023.

42   Mahita Gajanan, "'What You're Seeing . . . Is Not What's Happening.' People Are Comparing This Trump Quote to George Orwell," *Time*, July 24, 2018.

43   Hannah Arendt, "Truth and Politics," *The New Yorker*, February 25, 1967.

44   Andrew Gawthorpe, "Republicans Are Trying to Rewrite the History of the Capitol Attack. Don't Let Them," *The Guardian*, May 28, 2021.

INDEX

ABOUT
MARINER BOOKS

MARINER BOOKS traces its beginnings to 1832 when William Ticknor cofounded the Old Corner Bookstore in Boston, from which he would run the legendary firm Ticknor and Fields, publisher of Ralph Waldo Emerson, Harriet Beecher Stowe, Nathaniel Hawthorne, and Henry David Thoreau. Following Ticknor's death, Henry Oscar Houghton acquired Ticknor and Fields and, in 1880, formed Houghton Mifflin, which later merged with venerable Harcourt Publishing to form Houghton Mifflin Harcourt. HarperCollins purchased HMH's trade publishing business in 2021 and reestablished their storied lists and editorial team under the name Mariner Books.

Uniting the legacies of Houghton Mifflin, Harcourt Brace, and Ticknor and Fields, Mariner Books continues one of the great traditions in American bookselling. Our imprints have introduced an incomparable roster of enduring classics, including Hawthorne's *The Scarlet Letter*, Thoreau's *Walden*, Willa Cather's *O Pioneers!*, Virginia Woolf's *To the Lighthouse*, W.E.B. Du Bois's *Black Reconstruction*, J.R.R. Tolkien's *The Lord of the Rings*, Carson McCullers's *The Heart Is a Lonely Hunter*, Ann Petry's *The Narrows*, George Orwell's *Animal Farm* and *Nineteen Eighty-Four*, Rachel Carson's *Silent Spring*, Margaret Walker's *Jubilee*, Italo Calvino's *Invisible Cities*, Alice Walker's *The Color Purple*, Margaret Atwood's *The Handmaid's Tale*, Tim O'Brien's *The Things They Carried*, Philip Roth's *The Plot Against America*, Jhumpa Lahiri's *Interpreter of Maladies*, and many others. Today Mariner Books remains proudly committed to the craft of fine publishing established nearly two centuries ago at the Old Corner Bookstore.